Coming to You Wherever You Are

KIP PEGLEY

Coming to You Wherever You Are

MUCHMUSIC, MTV, AND YOUTH IDENTITIES

WESLEYAN UNIVERSITY PRESS

Middletown, Connecticut

Published by Wesleyan University Press, Middletown, CT 06459

www.wesleyan.edu/wespress

Printed in the United States of America

5 4 3 2 1

Library of Congress Cataloging-in-Publication Data

Pegley, Kip.
Coming to you wherever you are : MuchMusic, MTV, and youth
identities / Kip Pegley.
  p.   cm.
Includes bibliographical references and index.
ISBN-13: 978-0-8195-6869-4 (cloth : alk. paper)
ISBN-10: 0-8195-6869-4 (cloth : alk. paper)
ISBN-13: 978-0-8195-6870-0 (pbk. : alk. paper)
ISBN-10: 0-8195-6870-8 (pbk. : alk. paper)
 1. Music videos—Canada—History and criticism. 2. Music videos—
United States—History and criticism. 3. MuchMusic (Firm) 4. MTV
Networks. 5. Music and youth—Canada. 6. Music and youth—
United States. I. Title.
 PN1992.8.M87P44 2008
 791.45'3—dc22   2007049130

Contents

❧

Preface and Acknowledgments

Ideally, a researcher desires the participation of the informants representing the institutions under analysis. Unfortunately, I was unable to access MTV executives for comment on my research findings. Their lack of cooperation is not entirely surprising; previous researchers repeatedly have commented on MTV's refusal to participate in interviews.[1] Tom Shales of the *Washington Post* states: "As a business, MTV is run like a fortress . . . inquiries from the press during non-celebratory periods are met with chilling officious evasiveness and Byzantine bureaucratic obfuscation."[2] Such was also my experience trying to gain access to the station. Fortunately, my findings and interpretations of the data on MuchMusic and *Jyrki* are interwoven with rich responses from their executives. In particular, I thank my interviewees in Toronto, Marco Bresba, Sarah Crawford, Denise Donlon, David Kines, and Avi Lewis, and in Finland, Marko Kulmala, Olli Oikarinen, Erja Ruohomaa, Elli Suvaninen, and Kristiina Werner-Autio. Thanks also to my Finnish colleagues Taru Leppänen, Pirkko Moisala, and Erkki Pekkilä for helping me establish contacts with Finnish music television viewers. I owe much to my Finnish informants who were willing to participate in my interviews. Their comments and responses have been invaluable contributions to this research.

I am indebted to the Social Sciences and Humanities Council of Canada for their financial assistance throughout this research, to York University and Queen's University for supporting me during my fieldwork trips, and to Queen's for providing funding in the final stages of the book. My thanks to Jim Kippen and the Faculty of Music, University of Toronto, for support during my postdoctoral fellowship and my colleagues at the Queen's School of Music for their encouragement.

I am grateful to Rob Bowman and Beverley Diamond for their guidance with earlier drafts of the manuscript and to Doug Gifford for his patience and expertise as we analyzed the database. My thanks also to the series editors at Wesleyan University Press, Annie Randall and Harry Berger, for their helpful insights.

I am indebted to many people for their tremendous emotional support over numerous years: Mary Louise Adams, Jody Berland, Donelda Gartshore, Susan Fast, Kathy Higgs, Faye Ibbitson, Catherine Kellogg, Samantha King, Cindy Lusignan, Nancy Miller, Dorit Naaman, Carol-Lynn Reifel, Marta Robertson, Tanya Stambuk, Julie Salverson, Gordon Smith, and Claudette Trudeau. Julie L'Heureux, this time I owe you much more than a million, and Barbara Clarke, thank you for always being there on the other end of the phone. And to my parents, Fred and Myrtle Pegley, and to my brother Fred and sister-in-law Patricia, thank you. It has finally arrived.

Coming to You Wherever You Are

CHAPTER ONE

Introduction

❧

I was a teenager when I first felt, unconsciously, the power of music videos. This was in the mid-1980s in Halifax, Nova Scotia, at a time when my musical life seemed to be taking a fairly typical trajectory: I was studying music at university while playing my primary instrument, trumpet, as much as possible. In addition to my school ensembles, I played with a professional symphony as well as a local big band, sometimes leaving evening orchestra concerts, changing frantically en route to the next performance. I remember most vividly playing Friday-night orchestra concerts where the dress was "all black," meaning long black skirts and suits. On those nights I returned home late at night, went down to my basement, and turned on NBC's *Friday Night Videos*. I walked toward the television while I pulled off my restrictive long black clothing, put on my jeans and settled back for a few hours of the verboten music: Night Ranger, Peter Gabriel, Journey. I sat alone, with my legs hanging over the side of the chair, watching the videos intently. Subsequently I began to consume many hours of videos on MuchMusic, Canada's national music television station, and moved into a musical and gendered rebellion that I did not share with any of my family, friends, classmates, or professors. Not until graduate school did I have the opportunity to leave historical musicology for popular music studies and abandon scores of *Elektra* and *Lulu* for videos by Madonna and Janet. My private obsession for popular music, and music videos in particular, found its home in a new and developing discipline.

As I studied popular music in the 1990s, however, I once again found myself marginalized. My music video sources, particularly the Canadian programming, were often overshadowed within academic scholarship by one primary, and often presumed source: U.S.-based MTV. Many researchers, in fact, did not clearly distinguish between video providers, and MTV often became the default station. I knew, however, that American and Canadian music television stations were different, and that when I talked about music television with my American peers we were not always conversing about the same texts. Yet explaining the differences between those texts in any sort of quantifiable way seemed impossible.

At a 1998 media conference in Toronto, Ontario, the academic bias toward American music television stations was still clearly apparent. A presenter at the conference introduced her paper by stating that she would incorporate excerpts from both MTV[1] and Black Entertainment Television (BET); from the station logos indicated in the corner of the videos, however, it was evident that all of the examples were taken from BET. During the question period I asked the presenter about her video sources. Were these videos representative of BET's repertoire rather than MTV's? How do their rap repertoires differ? Is there a correlation between the stations and the racial identities their video repertoires construct?

The question did not receive the attention I expected and was quickly deflected to an audience member for a response. A young man explained to me that BET airs more "low-budget" videos, which, he intimated, would not be of high-enough quality to be aired on the high-priced and heavily produced MTV. The presenter agreed, and quickly moved on to the next question. I believe the audience member was correct. Yet, although I have heard this statement repeatedly, it remains for me only a partial explanation. Because of MTV's exclusive airing strategies, some videos shown on the station do not appear elsewhere; conversely, many videos aired on BET simply would not appear on MTV. Reasons for these omissions and inclusions, as I shall explain in the following pages, extend beyond budgetary constraints. They belong to a far more complex matrix of power than the audience member's explanation would allow.

Although I found the issue of station repertoires and their ideological implications unsatisfactorily addressed, the paper and discussion were progressive insofar as they brought attention to a station's repertoire, that is, a station other than MTV.[2] Because the conference was hosted in Toronto, however, it seemed slightly ironic that at no point during the discussion of video station repertoires did anyone reference the source most familiar to many of the local attendees present: Canada's MuchMusic. Reasons for the academic bias toward MTV are numerous: in addition to its wide distribution within the United States, MTVN (MTV Networks) has assertive international marketing strategies and a largely one-way distribution of popular culture. It is also the undisputed international video gatekeeper, with stations scattered from Asia to South America, and Europe to Australia, which, coupled with its ever-expanding list of servers, have raised justifiable concerns within music television literature regarding the network's aggressive media imperialization. Scholars have recognized that its cultural power has become ubiquitous.

One market, however—Canada—remains irritatingly elusive, and MTVN spokespeople repeatedly have expressed their frustration at their inability to permeate north of the forty-ninth parallel. From MTV's perspective, the challenges Canada poses exist on several levels. First, since 1984 Canada has had its own music video station, Toronto-based Much-Music. Second—and this relates to the first point—television licensing in Canada falls under the powers of the Canadian Radio-Television and Telecommunications Commission (CRTC), the policies of which forbid new stations to enter the market if they replicate existing Canadian offerings. To bypass these regulations, MTV joined forces with Calgary-based Craig Broadcasting; they attempted their first affiliation with a digital Canadian channel in the fall of 2001, giving them initial (although limited) access to Canadian cable subscribers. In 2005, MTV collaborated with CTV, Canada's largest privately owned, English-language television network. Together, they relaunched MTV Canada as a specialty channel devoted to talk programming. MTV Canada then expanded through a deal with Rogers Cable, Canada's largest cable service provider, making it accessible in several major urban centers. Despite such efforts, however, MTV is likely to be frustrated north of the border: as long as MuchMusic continues to satisfy the requirements of the CRTC and receive high viewer ratings, a full-fledged Canadian MTV (including music videos, interviews, and news) will take some time to reach Canadian viewers.

With the aid of such Canadian protectionist regulations, MuchMusic has worked quietly, yet aggressively, expanding in 1989 from a pay-television service to become part of most basic cable packages in Canada. Subsequently, the station established several additional English-language specialty music services, including MuchMoreMusic, a station launched in response to VH1 that serves an older demographic (airing some VH1 programs); other, more specialized stations available on satellite including Much Loud and Much Vibe (featuring "active rock" and urban videos respectively); two French-language stations (MusiquePlus and MusiMax); stations in the United States (MuchUSA), Argentina (MuchaMusica), Malaysia (MuchMusic Malaysia), and the Middle East (MuchMusic Arabia); as well as programming on Mexico's Once TV station (MuchMusic Mexico) and on Finland's largest commercial station (an after-school program entitled *Jyrki*).

The short history of MuchUSA evidences MuchMusic's successful international format. The station began as a joint partnership between

CHUM Limited (one of Canada's leading media companies and owner of MuchMusic), and American Rainbow Media Holdings.[3] At its peak, MuchUSA had 24 million subscribers in the United States. CHUM subsequently sold its interest in the channel to its partner in 2000, with the condition that in 2003 Rainbow Media would no longer have the rights to the MuchMusic name or programming. The station was renamed Fuse in April 2003. Critics subsequently complained that Fuse has been uncreative, becoming a slightly repackaged MuchMusic within an American context. Others complain that since its inception Fuse has "sold out," limiting their playlists to mostly alternative, punk, rock, and emo in an attempt to compete with MTV (which is more hip-hop–based) at the expense of variety and innovation.[4] In the midst of these criticisms, MuchMusic executives have expressed interest in relaunching an American music television station. Regardless of how successful this initiative turns out to be, MuchMusic has demonstrated that it clearly can compete internationally, making it one of Canada's paramount media outlets, both at home and abroad.

The absence of an MTV station from Canadian cable packages, while troubling for MTV, is less problematic for the many Canadians who intuit that MuchMusic—self-identified as "the nation's music station"—is in fact substantially different from MTV and a worthy source of music videos and popular culture. I for one have been among MuchMusic's supporters: my long-held perception, after years of viewing from my home in Canada and during my visits to the United States, was that MuchMusic consistently aired more videos than MTV and featured performers representing a wider range of races and ethnicities. MTV, by contrast, had always seemed less pluralistic and more restricted by its heavier (that is, more repetitious) video rotation schedule, resulting in a smaller number of videos and a narrower range of genres. The stations' contents—from their video repertoires to their televisual flows—seemed to construct different types of relationships with viewers; these relationships, in turn, contributed to what I perceived, following Benedict Anderson,[5] to be two distinct constructions of imagined national communities. Whereas the Canadians seemed to be addressed as a pluralistic collective, American viewers were distinguished by their unique individualism.[6]

Despite MuchMusic's distinctive appearance and its increasing international cultural influence, it has slipped under the radar and largely evaded critical attention in either academic or trade publications.[7] When MuchMusic *is* considered within these contexts, it is often described—briefly—as a noteworthy alternative to MTV. In a 1991 article for *Billboard*, for instance, Jim Bessman pointed to a number of important differences between the two stations, including MuchMusic's live format, its hyperactive open studio setting, and, perhaps most important, a wider video repertoire than that shown on MTV.[8] Citing what MuchMusic originator Moses Znaimer called a "more mature and broader" playlist, Bessman fully supported the claims that MuchMusic is distinctive from MTV in both repertoire and style. More recently, Jack Banks cited MuchMusic in his landmark book on MTV as a notable alternative to the American station, particularly for its attempt to "preserve and promote [Canada's] own artists and musical culture."[9] That MuchMusic might feature a televisual aesthetic that reflects Canadian as opposed to American cultural articulations has fallen on deaf ears, particularly among MTV's executives. MTV spokespeople have expressed their discontent with Canadian regulations, ignoring the possibility that MuchMusic serves Canadians more effectively than would their station. As Tom Freston, former MTV Networks Chairman and CEO put it, "It's easier for us to operate in Vietnam and Lebanon than it is to operate in Canada. Canada's about the only country in the world we have a problem operating with . . . if MTV is not bad for people in Poland, what's the problem with Canada?"[10]

What *is* the problem with Canada? Can we say with confidence that MuchMusic is different enough from MTV to suggest that it serves Canadians better than its American counterpart would? MuchMusic must meet minimum Canadian content regulations that stipulate Canadian television stations air a minimum amount of Canadian content.[11] Can we say then that their "more mature and broader" playlist includes legislated Canadian programming, or does it simply replicate the MTV rotation with a few Canadian videos added in? More broadly, does it attempt to construct a sensibility different from MTV's? If so, are MuchMusic's and MTV's differences nuanced by Canadian and American cultural aesthetics respectively, or are they simply indicative of two distinct North American stations competing for ratings?

In the next three chapters I explore these questions as I undertake a comparative critique of a 1995 sample of MuchMusic and MTV. I examine how the two stations contributed to and continue to construct our sense of national, gendered, and racial identities. I approach these questions by situating the stations as sites of "specificity," within what Elspeth Probyn calls "zones of possible forms of belonging."[12] These stations indeed present communities—both imagined and visible—to which people can relate (and in turn, belong) through their sense of what it means to be American or Canadian, to be part of a particular race or combination of races or ethnicities, or to be a gendered individual. While I recognize that these three parameters are connected and fluid, it is important to isolate these "specificities" and explore their individual, discursive problematics. What follows below is a brief discussion of my use of the terms "nationhood," "race," and "gender," as well as my criteria for a fourth categorizational system I shall use as a frame for my analysis: music video genres.

In my discussion of "nationhood," I differentiate between "state" (a sovereign political entity) and the "nation," which has been defined previously by Ernest Renan as a "moral consciousness," or "spiritual principle."[13] Whereas states have tangibility, nations do not. Instead, nations have narratives and iconography that emotionally bond groups of people (regardless of whether these people actually are citizens of a state). In this analysis, I avoid evoking an a priori set of homogeneous, cohesive, polarized images and narratives for "Canadian" and "American" national identities. As Ien Ang argues, trying to identify a pure national "essence" is, of course, both unrealistic and pointless. As she states, this attempt is

damagingly oblivious to the contradictions that are condensed in the very concept of national identity. Defining a national identity in static, essentialist terms—by forging, in a matter of speaking, authoritative checklists of Britishness, Dutchness, Frenchness, and so on—ignores the fact that what counts as part of a national identity is often a site of intense struggle between a plurality of cultural groupings and interest inside a nation, and that therefore national identity is . . . fundamentally a dynamic, conflictive, unstable and impure phenomenon.[14]

Communications scholar Richard Collins echoes Ang's concerns when he states that the idea of a national culture is a "mystifying category error" that is inherently self-contradictory.[15] Indeed, the racial, ethnic, religious, and linguistic diversity of countries such as Canada or the United States rightly frustrates attempts to construct a completely unified collective identity. It is important, however, to understand that discursively produced and socially negotiated narratives provide the foundation for Canadian and American nationhood. Because these two countries are wealthy nation-states, the perpetuation of these narratives takes on even more importance.

At times, Canadian identity—especially for those with hegemonic power—ironically is defined by the *lack* of a clear identity, which then empowers Canadians to frown upon such nation-states as the United States where nationhood is considerably more united (especially in times of national crisis). But forging a nation requires more than its citizens' identifying as "not American"; indeed, Canadians are also unified discursively on a daily basis by notions of a more gentle, polite, "feminized," and multiculturally tolerant society—particularly, again, in relation to the United States. More precisely, within the popular mainstream, cultural industries reinforce a notion of "Canadianness" that is inextricably linked with the powerful multicultural mosaic myth. I do not wish to argue here for the legitimacy, efficacy, or actuality of the "mosaic" in practical terms. But this trope nonetheless carries significant metaphorical meaning, shaping our cultural perceptions. Many Canadians celebrate and support the notion of the mosaic as a compensatory strategy that in turn makes them feel superior to their American peers.[16] Accordingly, minority traditions—and studies of those traditions—are supported in order to sustain the mosaic myth. As Eva Mackey argues, despite its democratic appearance, the celebration of Canada's minority populations can be read as an effective means for masking, protecting, and reifying relations of hegemonic cultural power.[17] Richard Day further suggests that the mosaic metaphor is also used to provide "substance" to this immense country, functioning "as the object of a desire for a Canadian identity that forever fails to achieve its goal, and thereby achieves its aim, which is to perpetuate itself."[18] I shall uncover throughout these pages a set of cultural narratives—like the multicultural narrative—that provide the stories and the emotional glue necessary to unite otherwise diverse groups of people. These narratives are inherently dangerous for two reasons. First, not all individuals or social groups will be accommodated in these narratives; the process therefore requires the inclusion of some stories and characters while simultaneously forgetting others.[19] Second, regardless of the narratives' structure or content, they will always function to benefit those who already possess hegemonic power.

Stuart Hall similarly has argued that identity is never entirely accomplished, but rather is always [re]constituted within representative modes.[20] Canadian identities, in that case, are never located in a fixed notion of the multicultural mosaic. They are constructed (like Canadian identity as a whole) through a complex matrix of cultural productions constantly in a process of reinvention. As part of the current study then, I explore which particular national narratives MuchMusic and MTV reinforce and how the stations contribute to the narratives' necessary instability and continued renewal.

As Tamar Mayer argues, it is impossible to understand a nation without understanding how integral gender and sexuality are to its definition: a nation "is comprised of sexed subjects whose 'performativity' constructs not only their own gender identity but the identity of the entire nation as well."[21] How artists "perform" their gender and how this performance in turn is conflated with nationhood will be a critical component of this analysis. Here I shall use "gender" to reflect the social constructions of "male" and "female." There are advantages and disadvantages to using this term. The advantage is in problematizing the biological essentialism (and subsequent determinism) that exists in "sex"; the disadvantage lies in masking the potential for gender as a performative continuum. This problem is particularly glaring in my discussions of the quantitative data that pertain to either "men" or "women," and I regret having to create these strongly delineated gender distinctions. Yet, as Judith Butler has noted, gender can also signify a unity of experience, a homogeneous category, if it is constructed in relation to an oppositional (heterosexual) gender system.[22] Throughout this analysis I shall move between these levels and refer to gender as both a unified set of representations ("men," "women,") and as an intersector with nationhood and race as points along a performative continuum. While recognizing that gender performances can range greatly, we should also note that gender coherence ultimately is mandatory for commodification within any media genre, including popular music (as long as it also encompasses the perception of social resistance, and the possibility of individual agency). In the context of MTV and MuchMusic, it is particularly important that gender appears to be consistent: the construction of nationhood hinges upon it. As Leslie Dwyer argues, for nationhood to appear as "natural," gender must be presented as essential and nonnegotiable. Only under these circumstances can nationalist constructs also be naturalized, a process that, in turn, further essentializes gender in a self-contained loop.[23]

Like gender, racist ideologies are also used to accomplish nationalist ideologies; as such, they are entwined within the fabric of state discourses and ideologies, thoroughly systematized therein, and often presented as unproblematic.[24] This systematizing is particularly true of multicultural policies: as Jo-Ann Lee and John Lutz have summarized, multiculturalism is deceptive; it may allow some citizens to feel a greater claim to a state over others, even though they may never actually be afforded full entry into it. Global migration shines a new light on racial relations and necessitates updating previously held notions of race and nationhood. "The emergence of mixed and multiple hybrid and hyphenated bodies as subjects and citizens, and postmodern discourses of hybridity and diaspora," they argue, "are additional challenges to old racial binaries of black and white."[25]

Stuart Hall correctly warns against classifying people based on genetic differences; he calls such classifying "the last refuge of racist ideologies."[26] Race is a nineteenth-century construction, and, as Hall rightly points out, it is a discursive, rather than biological category.[27] Hence, race should be seen first and foremost as cultural construct, one that plays a significant role in musical production, dissemination, and consumption. As Russell Potter has pointed out in his analysis of hip-hop, music continues to be one of the most powerful expressions of race.[28] Similarly, William Sonnega has argued that, within MTV circles, difference is almost exclusively relative to the color of an artist's skin.[29] I would argue that MTV and MuchMusic contribute significantly to binary black/white racial dichotomies through the musical genres they favor, although this relationship frequently is complicated (particularly on MuchMusic). Accordingly, in this analysis of music video stations, as with analyses of other representative forms, we must struggle to recognize race as a cultural construct while simultaneously problematizing it as such. We must uncover the *types* of racist discourses that are produced, and seek to understand what is to be accomplished through that production.

In the pages that follow, nationhood, gender, and race are examined and compared using a battery of video parameters ranging from filmic techniques to performance force (see appendix A). The most important of these parameters is music video genres. Strategies for categorizing genres, like those for the previous three axes, will always be incomplete because at least some of the subjective criteria for determining genres lie with the individual listener/viewer. Nonetheless, it is important to outline the criteria used for the current study in order to make the methodology transparent. As Simon Frith rightly has argued, one problem of genre categorization historically has been that the analysis of context took precedence over the text itself.[30] In an attempt to balance musical with extramusical signifiers, Roy Shuker since has identified three broad characteristics that should be considered when creating any genre classification: the musical traits, the nonmusical visual style, and the interactive relationship between artist and audience.[31] Following Shuker, I based my video genre criteria on all three parameters. To determine the genre, videos first were identified sonically (instrumentation, instrumental and vocal timbre, presence or absence of solos, and so on). Next, visual style of artists and the video overall were considered (the inclusion of "rockumentary" footage, the grain of the film, the artist's visual style, and so on). Finally, I took into account the performer/audience relationship as depicted within the video (size of audience and venue, proximity of audience to the stage, and so on.). Following these guidelines, I initially identified twelve musical genres:

rock
alternative
pop/rock
rap
urban
hard rock/metal
dance
folk/traditional and pop/traditional
punk
reggae
industrial
other

The "other" category included videos outside of the eleven defined genres. The word "other" was chosen deliberately to reflect the marginalization of these musics from the mainstream genres. While useful for some analyses, these categories were inappropriate for a large-scale overview like this one because there were too many groupings and the smaller categories (reggae, industrial) were, in the final analysis, rendered statistically insignificant. A second system was designed to reflect larger trends at the expense of genre specificity. Accordingly, the smaller genres were collapsed into one, arriving at a final grouping:

rock
alternative
pop/rock
rap
urban
other

The following is a broad-ranging description of these categories:

Alternative: A wide-ranging post-punk category, characterized by fairly abrasive guitar timbres (for instance, Nirvana's "grunge" sound). Artists are usually dressed-down relative to other musical genres and lyrics are often more socially critical and/or introspective than pop/rock lyrics. At least part of the musical performance (on- and/or offstage) is usually included in the video and the venue is usually midsize or small where the artist can appear close to her/his fans (examples from the current sample include Smashing Pumpkins, "Bullet With Butterfly Wings," and Pearl Jam, "Alive").

Pop/rock: Characterized by more tuneful, singable melodies, and "lighter" instrumental timbres, this genre usually is production-heavy. That is, the producer often has more control over the final sound than the artist. Instrumental musical performance is usually concealed within the videos and dance is foregrounded. "Live" performances in front of a delineated audience are not common (examples include Janet Jackson, "Runaway," and Mariah Carey, "Fantasy").

Rap: Rap is a declamatory, text-heavy genre with emphasis on electronic beats. Like pop/rock, instrumental musical performance is usually concealed in these videos and "live" performances usually include a small group of people rather than a formal "audience" per se (examples include Salt-N-Pepa, "Push It," and Queen Latifah, "Ladies First").

Rock: Characterized by vocals, electric guitars, bass, and drums with a strong backbeat. Instrumentation is most often shown in the videos, and the performance may take place within the context of the video's narrative, and/or within any size venue, often with a formal audience (examples include Aerosmith, "Janie's got a Gun," and Melissa Etheridge, "Your Little Secret").

Urban: Soul music of the 1980s and 1990s, this genre is melodic, characterized by smooth production techniques, and tends to conceal instrumental musical performance in the videos. As I shall outline in chapter 3, urban performances may take place within the narrative setting and/or in a more formal venue (for example, TLC, "Diggin' On You," and Boyz II Men, "I Will Make Love to You").

Other: A "catchall" category, including hard rock/metal, industrial, dance, and so on. Hard rock/metal occasionally is separated out from this category and discussed as a discrete genre characterized by grinding vocal and guitar timbres (power chords), often virtuosic guitar soloing, heavy drum sound, and emphasis on "live" performances (with audiences) in their videos.

All of these categories, of course, must continually be problematized; a single video may be placed within any number of classifications depending upon programming context and viewer decoding strategies. Some videos, for instance, could be categorized as either pop/rock or urban. As a result, musically ambiguous videos are identified according to the videos that proceed and follow it either within a general music video flow or within thematically organized programs.

This study uses as its basis a one-week simultaneous sample of the two stations, resulting in 336 hours of footage through which I analyzed their entire video repertoires.[32] That week, November 4–11, 1995, the two stations showed approximately 2,500 videos: MTV aired 248 different videos, most of which were repeated, resulting in 1,033 "video events";[33] MuchMusic aired 400 different videos, which, when repeated, resulted in a repertoire of 1,457 "video events."[34] But comparing stations exceeds looking at just the video content. It must involve a more holistic analysis of both the musical and extramusical components. To this end, I analyzed a battery of parameters for every video on both stations, and delineated a segment that was examined for its extramusical content. As part of this focused extramusical analysis, I documented everything that appeared between the videos from visual and sound trailers to commercials and station logos, all coded to the temporal level of the second. This process entailed the creation of a database into which these events—individual videos, commercials, trailers, and the like—could be coded and entered and, subsequently, extracted and interpreted.

Despite the inherent problems and challenges in understanding the relationships among nationhood, gender, race, and musical genre within only one week of programming, the endeavor is both worthwhile and timely for four important reasons. First, both stations have a significant international viewership. More regions of the world now receive MTV than those that don't, and, as outlined previously, MuchMusic has made itself well known both within Canada and on the international media scene. Yet, while MTV has received significant academic attention, MuchMusic has received little, and there is no comparative analysis of the two stations vis-à-vis identity construction. The present analysis will attempt to remedy that lack.

Second, the impact of music television on young viewers is considerable. MTV, for instance, is more than a music video outlet: it is a lifestyle channel that has been described as "a cultural presence, a way of understanding popular culture and the postindustrial, postmodern scene" for American youths.[35] My previous research within Canada corroborates that music television is also a significant presence on the other side of the forty-ninth parallel. In a 1990 study of preadolescent youths conducted at a Metropolitan Toronto intermediate school, female respondents reported watching an average of one-and-a-half hours of MuchMusic daily while the boys averaged more than three hours and these figures were increasing.[36] MuchMusic's target demographic is ages 12 to 34 with the most dedicated viewers between 18 and 24 (MTV's general viewership is also between 12 and 34, with a more dedicated group between 12 and 24 and the most dedicated viewers between 12 and 17, slightly younger than those who watch MuchMusic). Music television, "the most influential cultural product of the age,"[37] is a significant, yet undertheorized force in the lives of Canadian youths.

Third, as American media conglomerates increase their power and international influence, it is important to explore whether cultural differences on either side of the border *do* exist so that we can determine if Canadian articulations should be protected, or, if differences cannot be found, whether the border should be fully opened for American imports. This protectionism is part of a larger debate that has been argued in law courts for years. Take, for instance, the dispute over split-run magazines. Until the 1990s, the United States was prohibited from shipping "split runs"— American magazines that recycle editorial content wrapped around Canadian advertising, resulting in so-called Canadian editions—into Canada. *Sports Illustrated,* however, found a loophole in the 1965 legislation and transmitted their magazine over the border electronically via satellite to a printing plant in Canada; in December 1995, they were penalized with an 80 percent excise tax. Time Warner, the owner of that magazine, protested by taking Canada to the World Trade Organization Court. The court ruled in its favor. U.S. Trade Representative Charlene Barshefsky responded to the decision by stating: "We have no objection to the promotion by Canada . . . of national identity through cultural development. . . . But we object to the use of culture as an excuse to take commercial advantage of the United States, or as an excuse to evict American companies from the Canadian market."[38] It is amusing that Barshevsky's criticisms are directed against Canada, where domestic companies in the film distribution business are 85 percent controlled by Americans, and domestic magazines occupy a mere 20 percent of Canadian newsstands. Overall, the United States exports $620 million (U.S.) worth of books each year to Canada, which accounts for 41 percent of its total book exports. American TV programs, recordings, magazines, and books combined dominate annual sales within Canada upward of 95 percent.[39] Eviction, indeed. But if there are no Canadian narratives that should be displayed on our newsstands, no articulations that we might want to protect from American-dominated media, current protectionist policy should be abandoned. A comparison between MuchMusic and MTV, as I shall argue here, can tell us much about the presumed uniqueness of Canadian articulations and how music video outlets shape nationhood. Thus it can suggest whether the protectionist policy should be reified or finally struck down.

Fourth, while all Canadian media are important sites of cultural analysis and critique, my analysis is important because MuchMusic, a pervasive disseminator of popular culture, is particularly significant. As noted by television analyst Richard Collins:

Elites have long experienced a transnational "high culture" for which they have occasionally incurred the opprobrium of nationalists who have anathematized them as cosmopolitans. However, it is the contemporary pervasiveness of an international *popular* culture in and through which the masses are thought to construct their identities and aspirations *outside* the dominant political institutions of the nation-state.[40]

MuchMusic, the most important specialty station licensed in Canada since the early 1980s (and, one may argue, *the* most important station for young Canadians), has become vital to the consumption, circulation, and articulation of popular culture among youths. MuchMusic's increasing pervasiveness both within Canada and abroad, combined with its undeniable social influence, suggests that an in-depth analysis of how the station fosters the construction of identities—national, racial, and gendered—is now warranted.

The type of data collection and analysis used here falls under the rubric of "content analysis," a methodology that implements a set of procedures in order to draw inferences from a text.[41] Content analysis has played such a crucial role in communications studies that it has been labeled "the logical center of broadcasting research."[42] Despite the tremendous potential and benefits of this pervasive methodology, content analysis has innumerable shortcomings, many of which are located in the research design itself. As Brian Winston points out, one of the first crucial decisions for outcome reliability is sample size so that the results can be described with as few misrepresentations as possible.[43] Second, despite the most well intended and carefully planned research sampling and data coding methodology, content analysis inevitably has significant, often unseen pitfalls at the interpretive level. Dominic Strinati, using the example of content analysis of media gender roles, has pointed out a few such dangers:

> While content analysis can give some idea of what . . . representations look like at particular points in time, it fails to go beyond purely descriptive accounts. . . . Content analysis rests upon the claims that media representations are coherent and uniform, not ambiguous or contradictory, and that the sex role stereotypes presented by the media are clear and consistent, not complex and open to varying interpretations.[44]

Strinati raises an important point here: content analysis often fails to move beyond the surface descriptive level. Strinati rightly points to another common flaw at the interpretive level: the researcher's emphasis of quantitative over qualitative information and subsequent failure to tie results back to the larger societal power relationships that underlie these representations.[45] In other words, pointing to apparent imbalances in representation does nothing to help us understand the power relations underlying those imbalances, the social structures partially responsible for them, or how those dynamics could be addressed. Strinati's final warning surrounds the claims for content analysis' "objectivity"[46] and this illusion is indeed a seductive trap for researchers dealing with substantial numbers and figures.

To address the first concern of sufficient sample size, I examined the samples of all available existing studies of the two stations. The most substantial sample was Steven Williams's weeklong study of MuchMusic that served as the basis of his master's thesis.[47] Having the 1993 MuchMusic sample with which the current study could be compared, I found it appropriate to isolate a one-week sample here as well. Because my study comprises data from *two* channels, however, this sample is twice the size of Williams's.

After deliberating sample size, I needed to determine whether the sample would comprise discrete or continuous material. Video samples generally are either discrete—meaning specific programs are taped over a period of days, weeks, or months and examined as a set—or, conversely, continuous samples of an entire day, series of days, or a week.[48] I was not interested here in examining particular programs but rather the *range* of each station's programming. As such, a simultaneous continuous period of time was deemed most appropriate.

By the fall of 1995 it was essential to determine the most appropriate recording dates. The week of November 4–11, 1995, was chosen because it fell between two important events: Halloween and American Thanksgiving. The sample therefore reflected the seasonal programming of the stations without being overly skewed by images relating to either of these particular events. A seven-day sample, of course, is only a snapshot and, given the changeability of music video stations and video chart positions, this analysis reflects that particular week but less accurately the weeks following or preceding. After all, a video may enter the charts in heavy rotation and quickly drop to medium rotation, thus frustrating attempts to find consistencies across even a month of airtime.

Second, despite the relatively small sample size, this analysis can be defended and qualified by contextualizing it as what Probyn defines as an event of "singularity": "the minute description of the specificity of things, the 'adding to' directed not at 'adding up' to some totality but at a description of 'exclusive actuality': what emerges from what is said now, here, and nowhere else."[49] This is a moment in media history when television was the primary source of music videos and when MTV and MuchMusic were by far the most powerful distributors in the United States and Canada, respectively. Before North American teenagers began downloading on-demand videos from countries at home and abroad, MTV and MuchMusic were the two sources that shaped their lifestyle and their sense of themselves as a gendered and racially defined citizen of the United States or Canada. And, despite all of the considerable changes to these two stations, many of the representational patterns evidenced that week in 1995 still mirror Canadian and American popular styles located within other cultural forms today. This continuity suggests that these national-bounded patterns are pervasive and ongoing and that MTV and MuchMusic cannot be read simply as corporate-driven "pop" music stations. They are co-contributors to national cultural articulations.

Strinati's emphasis on the importance of moving an analysis beyond the descriptive level is well taken here. I appreciate his warnings against claims of uniformity and definitive interpretation. I address these problems in my analysis by moving from the general to the specific, from percentages and numerical patterns to the individual video. In more than one instance, moving between these two levels demonstrates (1) how the broad picture often is misleading, and (2) how various interpretations could result, depending upon the particular analytical focus and/or the individual decoding processes of North American music television viewers.

Another pitfall of content analysis concerns relating the numerical findings to larger social issues. Within this study I work from the data figures and move inward, from numbers to individual videos and back in order to tie my analysis into larger societal trends and imbalances. This is a quantitative/qualitative exploration that spills over the expected boundaries of both empirical, statistical interpretation and ethnographic probing. But such a mapping allows me to bring new issues into focus as I examine the powerful intersections/overlap/contradictions of race, gender, and nationality and how they intersect societal power structures.

In the chapters that follow I move between discussing broad video styles and analyzing individual videos in detail. In only a handful of these analyses do I discuss the directors or choreographers, the critical people "behind the scenes." These individuals do have considerable importance: as mentioned previously, government regulators like the CRTC determine "Canadian content" according to the nationality of the composer and location of the recording site, among other factors. For this analysis, however, I wanted to consider the final text as it was presented to viewers on music television stations. In 1995, music videos did not consistently include the name of the director at the beginning of the video (even today directors are not always named). Because I was interested in exploring what the viewer actually sees on the television screen—recognizing that some viewers keen to learn more about a video will seek out that information on their own—details on the origins of the video's message, the director, and the choreographer were not included in the present discussion. Some artists (usually those already established) have more control of the video's content than others; most often, however, the video's predetermined concept is given to the artist for her/him to perform. While many young viewers recognize that the video's message and visual style may not originate with the artist, most often these features are linked with the artist after the video is viewed. If Sarah McLaughlin were to perform in a video with a clear racist subtext, for instance, viewers would hold *her* responsible for the inappropriate message. While it is important not to assume that the images and sounds of the final text originated with the individual artist, the design, direction, message, and choreography, of course, are intended to tie in with the artist's existing—or desired—style and the musical genre he/she performs. Accordingly, I shall indicate when a video "features" individuals or groups rather than stating that a video is "by" those persons, allowing room for the tremendous role played by people other than the featured artists.

Finally, the issue of content analysis and research "objectivity" warrants attention. Admittedly, I, as well as innumerable other content analysis researchers, launched my project with preconceived ideas and expectations: I would not have found this research sufficiently compelling to serve as the basis of a book had I not anticipated that at least some of my assumptions regarding the stations' differences would be actualized. These assumptions were drawn from many sources, the two most important being (1) many hours of watching MuchMusic and MTV; and (2) a number of "intuitions" regarding differences between American and Canadian cultural articulations (which, of course, subsequently influenced my perceptions of the two stations). Such "intuitions" are, in fact, anything *but* intuitions. As a Canadian attuned to debates surrounding Canadian identity/ies, Canadian "difference" can be experienced at multiple levels, from government policy (for example, multiculturalism, legislated in Canada but not in the United States) to television programs (especially those produced by the Canadian Broadcasting Corporation) to more general public discourses. Further, Canada has a long history of legally recognizing its citizens' differences, from Anglophones and Francophones in its Official Languages Act, to religious rights as manifest in separate school boards, to the rights of the Quebecois in a separate civil code, and so on. Such differences often are not immediately visible or tangible for the American visitor or researcher but are felt and experienced by many Canadians on a daily basis. Admittedly the questions asked and data that follow are filtered vis-à-vis these perceptions and experiences. Occasionally my findings confirmed my assumptions; at other times they shattered them. Perhaps most important, I have attempted to go beyond nationalist binaries to uncover the numerous contradictions and inconsistencies that threaten to destabilize Canadian and American nationalist imaginaries.

That the sample was recorded in 1995 deems this a historical study; numerous music television parameters have changed significantly since that time. First, music television increasingly has relied less on music videos and more on series programming with lifestyle shows like *The Real World, Jackass,* and *The Osbournes.* This shift was important because music video shows, which are categorized as "short" programming, usually achieve less than 1 percent ratings, whereas longer-format shows, which air for thirty minutes or more, receive higher viewer ratings for longer periods.[50] This increased viewing time, of course, is critical for advertising revenue because ratings systems often did not register viewing practices under a half hour in length. As a result, viewers today are consuming a different type of programming than that shown when the stations began in the 1980s (or even in 1995).

Today's viewers, however, are not consuming MTV and MuchMusic just to learn about new music videos. In a recent "MTV Deprivation Study," fifty committed MTV watchers promised to give up MTV and not connect with MTV.com for one month to see what they would miss most about the station. The results, according to Betsy Frank, executive vice president for research and planning at MTV Networks, were astounding: "Some people dropped out. Others felt alienated because they were deprived of a certain medium. They felt at a social disadvantage compared to their peers because they couldn't join in conversations. They didn't know much about new movies coming out."[51] It is noteworthy that Frank reported the viewers' overall loss of connection to popular entertainment. Clearly, MTV's heavy viewers value the station as an important source of lifestyle information, including music videos as part of the package.

The second significant change over the last decade is that music television is no longer the sole source of videos; in fact, it is increasingly a secondary video source. Viewers now turn to the Internet for videos-on-demand where they can download music onto computers and MP3 players. User-generated sites, including social networking Web site MySpace, photo-sharing site Flickr and video site YouTube have lured the public away from television viewing into their own interactive networks. YouTube is the most threatening site to the ongoing success of music television: here users can upload private video recordings, bootlegs, and recorded commercial videos. User enthusiasm has made this an extremely popular site in a very short time span: as of early 2007 it received hits from 20 million unique users per month who download 100 million downloads per single day.[52] Instead of fighting online music sites like YouTube, MTV and MuchMusic both have invested considerable time and attention in Web sites (MTV.com and MuchMusic.com) in order to complement and enhance their offline services. MTV Networks also has launched MTV Urge (a new digital downloading service), Overdrive (a broadband television network that offers on-demand programming including new music videos and additional footage from MTV shows), and will soon offer Flux (a replacement for their VH2 station that will feature music videos complemented by user-generated content). American viewers will be able to access Flux's blog via their cell phones and interact with other viewers via the Web site. From all of these changes it is clear that music television is going through another metamorphosis, much like when it began in 1981, although this time it will be a considerably more interactive medium. If MTV and MuchMusic are to survive, they simply will have to adapt to users' desire for on-demand content and interactive capabilities.

Since the mid-1990s MTV's geographical specificity has also shifted in an attempt to make the stations more locally relevant. Whereas Canada's MuchMusic has always been visibly located in downtown Toronto, MTV began by placing VJs (video jockeys) in a decontextualized loft with no inflections that would give away its actual location. MTV's move to its Times Square studios in the late 1990s created a new sense of temporal and physical situatedness for the network, particularly through its daily request program, *Total Request Live* (TRL). This flagship program features frequent shots of the New York cityscape and the ever-present crowd of screaming teens gathered on the street below. Large windows encase the studio itself and VJs are surrounded by a live studio audience, resembling MuchMusic's interactive format. Times Square has become the MTV parallel to Toronto's Queen Street.

Despite all of these changes, however, an exploration of MTV and MuchMusic's 1995 content remains relevant to us today. First, these stations are still extremely critical disseminators of popular culture: Much-Music, as noted previously, now serves many regions internationally, and MTV reaches more than 412 million households in 164 territories worldwide (and it still has the highest television ratings among viewers 12 to 34). These figures, of course, include a significant population without Internet access, many of whom will not have access to it in the near future. MTV will remain for many international viewers a *television* station with significant cultural influence.

Although this work examines the content of both stations, the reader will undoubtedly be aware of my emphasis on MuchMusic. Reasons for this are twofold. First, as mentioned previously, while there are numerous exceptional books that address music videos' structure and dissemination within the music industry, particularly vis-à-vis MTV, MuchMusic's programming has largely been excluded from the scholarly literature.[53] Second, stemming from this paucity of scholarly attention, I have approached this project as an exploration of how MuchMusic helps shape the Canadian musicocultural industry. Using a parallel American station like MTV as a comparative backdrop is thoroughly justifiable. As Morley and Robins have pointed out in their analysis of "European culture," analyses of cultural identities are best not undertaken in isolation:

Rather than analyzing cultural (or national) identities one by one and then, subsequently (as an optional move) thinking about how they are related to each other (through relations of alliance or opposition, domination or subordination), we must grasp how these "identities"...are only constituted in and through their relations to one another. . . . "European culture" is seen to be constituted precisely through its distinctions from and oppositions to American culture, Asian culture, Islamic culture, etc. Thus, difference is constitutive of identity.[54]

Nowhere is the phrase "difference is constitutive of identity" more poignant than in analyses of Canadian-American cultural distinctions and shared articulations. MuchMusic is part of a cultural infrastructure within a country that embraces, criticizes, and usually resents American popular cultural imports; it can be thoroughly understood only if it is considered relative to what it absorbs and/or rejects from the ubiquitous American music television industry. One means of exploring MuchMusic's construction of identity difference, as Philip Schlesinger might argue, is by examining the means by which it creates boundaries: "Identity is as much about exclusion as it is about inclusion, and the critical factor for defining the ethnic group therefore becomes the social *boundary* which defines the group with respect to other groups."[55] How MuchMusic establishes boundaries that continually reconstitute a sense of cultural difference is paramount not only to understanding the station, but to understanding the larger process of how Canadian popular media create a uniquely defined culture, in part, to ensure their own survival.

My analysis will be divided as follows: in chapter 2, "It's All Just Fluffy White Clouds," I target the stations' extramusical content. Here Much-Music and MTV are compared and contrasted vis-à-vis their televisual flows (the entire televisual content) after which I examine the stations' extramusical similarities and differences and how this results in unique constructions of "imagined" nation-bound communities. Borrowing from the work of Harold Innis and Jody Berland,[56] I conclude by considering how the stations' differences reveal their disparate media biases in constructing space, time, and identity for viewers on either side of the border.

In chapter 3, "'Simple Economics': Images of Gender and Nationality," I explore the connections among women, instrumentation, and nationhood by targeting how women's instrumental performances differ on the two stations. I then examine Canadian and American celebrity constructions as they are manifest within the performance contexts and synthesize how all of these parameters tie into existing national narratives of what it means to be gendered as a "Canadian" or an "American." In chapter 4, "Multiculturalism, Diversity, and Containment" I explore how the stations expanded their repertoires in the 1980s and 1990s to establish unique, carefully controlled, nationally inflected relationships between dominant and marginalized musical traditions. Using examples by Euro-American and African diasporic performers, I examine how multiculturalism appears to be "celebrated" on MuchMusic and MTV while Western and non-Western representations are negotiated such that ethnocentric norms—which pervade North American cultural media—are never contested.

Arriving at divisions for chapters 3 and 4 was not a simple or straightforward process. Recognizing that it is valuable to address nationality, gender, and race as individual social constructions, each warranting its own chapter, it is also critical to examine them as linked and dependent constructions. To that end, I foreground the results of my analysis of individual video components within a specific chapter, but cross-relate them across these axes. My rationale for placing the analyses of the video components within a particular chapter is based on quantifiable differences pertaining to one of the three axes (nationality, gender, or race) more so than it does to the other two. For instance: as part of the analysis I examined the frequency with which women appeared as instrumentalists as opposed to vocalists on the two stations. According to the data, these imbalances are largely the result of gendered, rather than racial considerations; accordingly, it is included in chapter 3 (gender). Conversely, my analysis of performing force (solo artist, duo, group, with or without backup instrumentation, and so on) suggests that while the frequency with which white female performers appear is fairly consistent on both stations, the frequency with which black "girl groups" appear on the two stations is strikingly dissimilar. These data arguably could have been placed in either the analysis of gender or race. Because the data pertain to only one segment of the female population—black females—it is examined primarily within my consideration of racial differences, but with offshoots to argue its significance in the constructions of gender as well as nationality.[57]

Having established many critical differences between the two domestic stations within chapters 2 through 4, I then examine their international marketing strategies. In chapter 5, "MuchMusic and MTV: The Finnish Context," I analyse how the stations reshape international markets, musical scenes, and viewers' relationships to place through a case study of Finland where the two are in direct competition. MTV Nordic, which had an important place in Finnish media in the 1990s, was joined in 1995 by *Jyrki*, an after-school program using MuchMusic's brand and format. Here I explore local and global tensions in music video dissemination, consumption and production practices, and how these result in fluctuating cultural boundaries and new electronic landscapes for Finnish youths. In chapter 6, initial assumptions are both confirmed and challenged as I synthesize my findings.

Over the next five chapters, I define, examine, and theorize on a plethora of video parameters. Taken individually, each of these parameters is limited when trying to interpret how music video stations construct racial, gendered, or national identities. When viewed as linked and dependent pieces of larger structural patterns, however, they evidence how popular media function on powerful ideological levels. Music videos, like any cultural texts, do not provide stable meanings: they are always fluid, negotiable, and contestable. Nonetheless, the video repertoires for one week in late 1995 wove a complex web of "preferred meanings," which, as Ien Ang has noted, are ideologies that "tend to support existing economic, political and social power relations."[58] It is MuchMusic's and MTV's "preferred meanings" that are explored in this study, meanings that are sewn together throughout the stations' visual and sonic features, from the singular, isolated video to the extended concert footage, and, significantly, everything in between.

CHAPTER TWO

"It's All Just Fluffy White Clouds"
The Extramusical Imagined Communities

Music television analyses often are designed to ask pointed questions of the video repertoires. Do the repertoires portray women and men in fixed and limiting roles, or are genders evidenced in empowering ways across genres? How do their repertoires represent racialized bodies? Before I explore the answers to these questions on either side of the forty-ninth parallel I shall contextualize the station's video repertoires by focusing on a facet of music television that has received little critical attention: the extramusical content. With few exceptions there is no careful consideration of the programming, the VJs, the visual and sound trailers, commercials, station identification tags, and the like, and how these components participate in establishing a station's relationship with the viewer so that the station can do its ideological work.[1] My exploration here targets MuchMusic's and MTV's stylistic distinctiveness and content discrepancies, the sum of which, I shall argue, contribute to the construction of different nationally inflected imagined communities. Several parameters in particular contribute to these constructions; I begin with an analysis of the stations' programming grids and means of disrupting "household flow"; that is, as defined by Rick Altman, the actual living practices of the person.[2] As Altman argues, television's sound component is intentionally designed to interrupt household flow and redirect our attention to the television set. In this chapter I explore how the stations bring our attention back to the program being aired and how these practices contribute to the manufacturing of different viewing communities. I then move on to explicate the role of the VJs, guest artists, video repertoires and commercials, and how they contribute to imagined alliances. I conclude by summarizing the stations' overall differences at the intersection of media biases and nationhood.

Considering the movement toward media globalization over the last decade, it might seem slightly surprising that television stations remain so decidedly nation-bound. As Ien Ang points out, "the categories of national identity and national culture are invested with formal, discursive legitimacy and are . . . dominantly used as a central foundation for official cultural and media policies."[3] Such may be even more true today than when this sample was taken in 1995. In the days and weeks following September 11, 2001, music television stations became important portals through which audiences and media tried to make sense of the attacks, defined "us" and "them" and solidified unified national positions from which "we" spoke. The ability to observe nation-based ideological constructs pre-9/11 goes far in helping us critique current ideological practices (some of which have intensified recently because of the need for national support during an unpopular war in Iraq). We have long been constructed throughout our media as unified imagined communities of Canadians and Americans, and nowhere is this more crucial in our age of increasing international uncertainty than on such seemingly natural and untainted youth-oriented stations as MTV and MuchMusic. In this chapter I expose some of the deeply embedded ideological mechanisms on these stations and illuminate how they were relevant to audiences from 1995 and continue to be today.

Programming

First, and at the most basic level, the stations' televisual styles can be differentiated by comparatively examining their programming grids. These distinct styles were evidenced more than twenty-five years ago when Raymond Williams attempted to identify differences in flow on public versus commercial television stations. When program content, one parameter of televisual flow, was examined according to the daily "listings," Williams noted that the evening sequences of the public broadcasting stations moved between disparate themes, from war dramas, to news, to regional programming on agriculture, and so on. These segments demonstrated the sharpest mood contrasts. The commercial stations, meanwhile, featured programs that were more thematically related, thus fostering a homogenized mood and, ideally, capturing the viewers' sustained attention.[4] According to Williams's research, the programs aired on public broadcasting were more likely to be selectively viewed as opposed to those shown on commercial television where the viewer was encouraged not to turn off the television set.

Implementing Williams's model of analyzing programming relative to thematic genres, I turn to the present sample to examine how MuchMusic's and MTV's thematic programming compare. There are a number of ways in which one could compare and contrast the thematic content of different shows on music television stations. The most obvious means organization by musical genre. Accordingly, as I outlined in the introduction, I settled upon six musical genres, including (from the largest to the smallest category), rock, alternative, pop, rap, urban, and "other" videos, and charted their programming over an average twenty-four-hour period.[5] On both stations, musical genres sometimes were featured exclusively (alternative videos, for example, were shown as a separate block on MTV's *Alternative Nation* and MuchMusic's *The Wedge*); more often, however, genres were combined with either related genres (rap with urban, for instance), or within the general video flow.

Programming flow *

I begin my analysis with MTV on the top left (0:00 designates 12:00 midnight). From midnight to 7:00 A.M., alternative, rock, and, to a lesser degree, rap and pop/rock dominated MTV, creating a seven-hour block. At 7:30 A.M., urban and rap were the most frequently heard genres on the show *Most Wanted Jams;* the music shifted back to rock, pop and urban from 8:00–10:00A.M. At 10:00 A.M. another break occurred: *MTV Jams,* which aired from 10:00 A.M. to 12:00 noon, combined urban and rap videos. From 12:00 noon to 15:00 (3:00 P.M.) the general video flow featured alternative music, mixed with rock and some rap. Between 16:00 and 17:30 (4:00 and 5:30 P.M.) on the weekends, urban and rap dominated (during the week this time slot featured mostly syndicated shows); after 17:30, the programming became mixed and video rotation became lighter as other syndicated shows were introduced into the flow (*Singled Out, Road Rules,* and so on).

There were both similarities and differences found in MuchMusic's programming. From midnight until 1:30 A.M. there was a mixture of alternative, rock, urban, and some "other" videos. At 1:30 A.M. however, we encountered a series of genre "surges": half-hour shows featuring rap (the program *Rap City*), alternative (*The Wedge*), and metal (*Power 30*) followed by a grouping of "other" videos. Between 4:00 and 5:30 A.M., rock was the most prominent genre heard in the flow.

At 6:00 A.M. there was a surge of pop rock, but this video grouping needs to be differentiated from the others. It represented the show *French Kiss,* which featured all French-language videos. These were not mainstream North American pop videos. They were in French and featured

---

* Two color figures representing MTV and MuchMusic's programming flow can be accessed at www.wesleyan.edu/wespress/mtvmuch.pdf

mostly Quebecois artists who were generally not Top 40 performers on English stations. The argument I am making here is that English-speaking viewers of pop/rock shows may or may not have been drawn to this half hour show; I believe it indicated a definite break from the rock videos that preceded it. From 6:30 to 10:00 A.M., rock and alternative dominated and from 10:30 to 11:30 "other" and rock videos were aired most often. A surge at 11:30 A.M. representing *French Kiss* stands alone again. Between 12:00 and 16:30 (noon to 4:30 P.M.), rock and alternative once again dominated for what may be viewed as one of MuchMusic's longest thematic periods of four-and-a-half hours. From 16:30 to 18:30 (4:30 to 6:30 P.M.) the genres changed quickly and decisively. At 19:00 (7:00 P.M.) the music news show *Fax* was aired, followed by one final mix from 19:30 to 22:30 (7:30 to 10:30 P.M.) with rock and alternative leading once again.

According to this analysis, MTV's programming underwent seven significant thematic changes per day whereas MuchMusic, because of its numerous genre shifts, underwent seventeen. Temporally, the airtime segments on MTV were thematically longer with less "interruption" from other genres, thus discouraging the interested viewer from turning the channel. MTV, then, reflected and extended the dominant American commercial model identified by Williams that encourages homogenization of both televisual content and the viewing audience. MuchMusic, meanwhile, more closely resembled the early public broadcasting model developed in Britain and Canada in which viewing was intended to be more selective. MuchMusic targeted disparate audiences made aware of one another as their programs collided in the daily listings, particularly at the half-hour level. As a result, MuchMusic's viewers were constantly informed of the plurality of their imagined community in contrast to MTV viewers, who were more often reminded of viewer similarities and shared musical tastes.

I do not mean to suggest that selective viewing is entirely reliant upon programming shifts. People watch television—and especially music video programs—in highly distractible ways. Music videos often play in the background while viewers talk on the phone, complete their homework, or do household chores. All the same, it is more likely that viewers/listeners will turn off a program if it sharply contrasts with what came before it (if the programming changed from heavy metal to pop music, for instance). Conversely, if a musical genre remains consistent for longer periods of time (an hour to several hours), a fan of that music is less likely to turn the station—especially if it is used as "background" entertainment.

Household flow

The second critical televisual discrepancy between the two stations after programming flow involves the manipulation of household flow. As Altman has pointed out, the sound component of television is responsible for interrupting our everyday lives (our "household flow") and redirecting our attention to the television. The soundtrack is largely responsible for luring us back to the television set and enticing us not to turn off the set altogether. Interrupting household flow is critical to the highly competitive station for one simple reason: ratings systems. Nielsen Media Research, the most internationally recognized television ratings system, for instance, assigns to individual members of a household a personal viewing button so the firm can track who is watching television at any one time (this monitoring is supplemented with diaries, phone conversations, and the like). The assumption is that when the television set is on a particular station the viewer is likely watching. Research firms recognize, of course, that such is not necessarily the case. Intermittent viewing is also probable while people cook in the kitchen or do their homework. But because rating systems are most concerned with tracking the operation of television sets and because stations seek high ratings for advertising dollars, it is in the best interests of the networks for viewers to keep the television set on, even if the viewer is not watching. Both stations, then, attempt to interrupt our household flow and repeatedly draw us back into the televisual image. Here I shall consider six means they use to do so: sound and visual trailers, silence, station identification tags, the use of direct address, the extended video format, and the presence or absence of VJs.

Trailers are announcements of programs, videos, or events to be aired at a future date. The use of trailers, Raymond Williams notes, was a result of intensified competition, when broadcast planners wanted to "capture" the audience and keep them watching their particular channel for upcoming events or events later that day, week, or month. Their use has differed among stations and countries. "In conditions of more intense competition, as between the American channels," Williams argues, "there is even more frequent trailing, and the process is specifically referred to as 'moving along,' to sustain what is thought of as a kind of brand loyalty to the channel being watched."[6]

For the current study I took the extramusical sample and coded both stations' trailers; that is, announcements of events to be shown in the immediate future, later that same day, in the upcoming week, and later that month. Trailers were either visually based (written text, usually accompanied by music), or reinforced with a voiceover by the VJ or a non-VJ. Table 2.1 outlines the number and types of trailers used by the two stations during one week.

Table 2.1

MTV's and MuchMusic's Visual and Sound Trailers

	MTV	MuchMusic
Number of trailers	89	87
VJ Voiceover	57	51
Non-VJ Voiceover	32	30
Without Voiceover	0	6

From table 2.1 we learn that a total of thirty-six trailers without a VJ were aired on MuchMusic; six did not carry a voiceover component at all. *All* of MTV's trailers had a textual component. This component points to a high degree of household flow disruption because the trailers used a voice to prompt the audience back to the screen. As Altman points out, for the interruption of household flow to be effective "there must be a sense that *anything really important* will be cued by the sound track." If sound cues are absent, the viewer is less compelled to pay attention.[7] Those six without an aural text on Much-Music were significant because they risked losing the viewer to other household activities. The same principle applies to the videos themselves, and a difference also was recorded here. The week of the sample, every one of MTV's videos included lyrics while MuchMusic aired six instrumental videos. I would argue that for many viewers, lyric "sound cues" prompt them to look at the singer to share the musical experience, particularly if they are singing along. These six videos, evidence of MuchMusic's expanded repertoire (including nonmainstream songs), risked losing the audience to other household activities and thus jeopardized the viewer-television connection.

While musical sounds and voices draw the listener into the televisual flow, the absolute lack of sound (a "dead track") is also able to prompt viewers' attention. As Joseph Boggs points out, within the filmic context the "dead track" provokes us to pay even more attention to the visual stimulus. With sounds in film so "naturalized," their absence actually creates tension; we await the next sound so that we can relax.[8] I would argue that music video dead tracks similarly fulfill the function of creating tension and encouraging attention.

A noteworthy difference in the use of absolute silence existed between the two stations. On MuchMusic, absolute silence was used in fifty-six videos, usually at the beginning, simultaneous with the visual narrative but before the music track began. These fifty-six videos combined constituted 3.8% of the repertoire. On MTV, however, ninety-five videos incorporated this technique, or 9.2% of their video repertoire. This means that an average of 5.5 *more* videos interrupted household flow daily on MTV than

MuchMusic by means of absolute silence, thus contributing to MTV's overall pattern of attracting listeners' attention back to the station.

A third means of interrupting household flow was accomplished through station identification tags. Tags feature station logos as the focal point of the visual image. Their objective is to present these logos in as many different and interesting forms as possible. MuchMusic's station tags featured a stationary *M* symbol that was invariably featured throughout the entire clip. The logo either changed colors or "shimmered" over the duration of the tag to hold the viewer's interest. Some sort of sound (a conga drum, say, or a bass beat) usually accompanied this logo. The image and sound were usually static and nondeveloping.

Like MuchMusic's practice, some of MTV's tags featured their logo (a large *M* with an embedded *tv*) in the opening frame. Here, the logo remained stationary and provided a great deal of color, although not much action. Most often, however, MTV incorporated the logo into a mini-narrative whereby it emerged only at the end of the clip. One ten-second animated tag featured a man seated in a dentist's chair while the dentist pulls his tooth; when turned upside down, it is revealed to be the MTV logo. In another, animated characters with protruding neck veins are shown straining; there is a sound of something being released, and the logo falls into toilet water. These mini-narratives are intended to engage the viewer; we watch and wonder when and how the logo will emerge. These narratives are usually accompanied by sounds, if not by words: sounds of splattering or popping draw us into the plot. MTV's narrative techniques were more purposeful and designed to keep us watching for the logo to emerge while simultaneously drawing us into the slightly raw, and usually humorous, aesthetic. In short, they were specifically designed to pique our interest and encourage us to continue watching until the narrative's conclusion.

The viewers' relationship to household flow was also shaped by particular modes of televisual address. All VJs on both stations engaged in direct address with the viewer; that is, they looked directly into the camera. Visiting celebrities on MTV also engaged in direct address with the viewer. On MuchMusic, however, the celebrities looked at the VJ or the audience, but never at the camera. This discrepancy is significant. When celebrities on MTV looked into the camera, it was as if the viewer was being "summoned." As Kurt Danziger notes, direct address is "another way of calling [the viewer]."[9] The viewer, in turn, was encouraged to reciprocate with equal intimacy and attention; this reciprocation again pulled us back to the television. On MuchMusic, however, we were not addressed directly by the stars. We were thus enabled to listen without being visually "called in," possibly allowing us to continue with our household activities more easily. This use of direct/indirect address also points to different modes of celebrity construction on the two stations; I shall return to this point later.

Losing the viewer to household flow was also risked more frequently on MuchMusic because they occasionally aired longer videos. While MTV consistently aired the standardized video length, MuchMusic included a number of longer songs including Barnes and Barnes's "Fishheads" (4:40) and Passengers' "Miss Sarajevo" (5:59). By extending the standardized video length, MuchMusic risked losing the attention of those viewers more accustomed to shorter videos with more formulaic structures.

Finally, the two stations' household flow strategies differed relative to the presence or absence of VJs. VJs play an important role beyond the function of simply announcing upcoming events. Andrew Goodwin argues that when the television personality is not present (for instance, on stations like Juke Box), a clear station identity cannot be made.[10] Following Danziger's assertion that direct address invites the viewer to reciprocate by looking back, I would also argue that when the VJ is absent from a show, leaving the viewer with only the sound of voice-overs, the audience is likely to watch the television set differently. The week of the sample, MTV aired only one show without a VJ: *Best of the 90s*. However, this program featured a split screen allowing viewers to write online communications that appeared underneath the video images (entitled *Yack Live*). This opportunity for interaction arguably made viewers attend to the visual image even *more* attentively than usual as they simultaneously watched the video and the commentary about the video and artist. All other shows on MTV featured VJs. MuchMusic, however, aired two shows the week of the sample without a VJ: the *MuchMusic Top 20 Countdown* (with a voice-over by VJ Bill Welychka but no visual image of him) and *Rap City* for four of the five shows (the show was "under construction" and in search of a new VJ). As such, the viewers were less likely to be drawn back visually to the television set when videos were being introduced.

While each of these discrepancies between the two stations individually may seem unavailing, their sum contributes significantly to our understanding of how they established their televisual flow. That MTV engaged in a higher level of flow is not surprising. As Altman notes, "flow is related . . . to the commodification of the spectator in a capitalist, free enterprise system"; in highly competitive markets, networks, because of their open competition for viewers, engage high levels of flow, while public stations work at much lower levels.[11] High degrees of flow also parallel more developed ratings systems; nowhere is this more clearly evidenced than in the United States. Within Canada, commercial stations similarly engage in extremely competitive modes, yet MuchMusic's degree of flow, while higher than that of most other Canadian stations—including both music and nonmusic services—resisted imitating the competitive American commercial model. It could be argued that MuchMusic, while undisputedly commercial, was inflected with the public broadcasting ideology—a pervasive model in Canada perpetuated largely by the Canadian Broadcasting Corporation—which attempted to serve a wide demographic of Canadian viewers of varying styles and tastes.

From the varied programming on the half-hour level to fewer audience demands to return their attention to the set, MuchMusic did not match MTV's American-style coefficient of network flow. I now turn to the function of VJs and guest artists, the video repertoire, and station commercials, and assess their contributions to the formation of distinct national communities.

In Front of the Camera: VJs and Celebrities

The function of the VJ has received little attention within academic scholarship. To address this paucity, Andrew Goodwin has pointed out a number of ways in which the VJs serve to "anchor" the MTV text. Of particular interest here is his argument that the VJs serve as persons with whom the viewer can identify, providing the familiar, friendly component against the backdrop of the superstars (the unreachable).[12] As part of his analysis, Goodwin references John Langer's article "Television's Personality System" (1981). Langer, borrowing from film analysis, argues that the models used to understand the construction of film stars, while useful for television, must be modified because there are distinct differences between the film and television celebrity. The film star traditionally has been separated out from our everyday lives; we exit our daily routine to view a film that appears to us "larger than life" onscreen. In addition, we often do not know when the star will release another film until we see it advertised. They appear, as Langer writes, within the realm of "the spectacular, the inaccessible, the imaginary."[13] In contrast, television's personality system is structured in opposition to that of film. "Good television," according to Langer, "personalizes whenever it can, rarely using a concept or idea without attaching it to or transforming it through the 'category of the individual.'"[14] In other words, it is the television personality that mediates television codes and transforms its symbolic discourses. It is through these personalities that events on television are "encoded" and "made intelligible," allowing the medium to operate ideologically.[15] Correlating ideas or opinions with television personalities requires that the TV personality be more reliable, consistent, and familiar than the film star. Television personalities should be predictable and somewhat regular; ideally, they should be scheduled at the same time each day or week.

During the selected week MTV featured twenty-two different VJs, eight regularly scheduled VJs and fourteen guests. A list of VJs and their respective programs appears in table 2.2.

Each of the regular VJs or guest VJs appeared on their own, in combination with another person, or both. On MTV, regular VJs often were associated with a particular genre and/or time of day. VJ Simon Rex, for instance, appeared on the general video flow program called *Music Videos*, and the show *Most Wanted*. Because VJs took turns hosting *Music Videos*, the viewer was never sure if Rex would appear on this program, but he always appeared on his own prime-time show *Most Wanted*. John Sencio, in addition to his appearances on *Music Videos*, appeared daily on the morning show *Rude Awakening* and Erik Palladino was the nightshift VJ appearing exclusively on the program *Dreamtime*. Time-specific shows (that is, programs while the world sleeps or awakens) were possible on MTV because they prerecorded their segments in a decontextualized, timeless loft setting and showed them at the same time of day across the United States. Accordingly, someone in Miami saw John Sencio on *Rude Awakening* at 6:00 A.M. Eastern, and a viewer in Los Angeles saw him at 6:00 A.M. Pacific time. The VJ appearances were temporally consistent and reliable, thus creating the impression that they were more familiar (and, as a result perhaps even more trustworthy). This familiarity was accomplished—as in the case of newscasters—without disclosing personal information about themselves to the audience. Even so, as Langer has pointed out, it is not necessary for the personalities to convey personal information about themselves in order to be received as familiar and accessible; every time a personality appears, even if he is not conveying personal information, he is still contributing to a "knowable" self.[16] Whereas stars play "parts," someone new and possibly unfamiliar each time we see them, personalities play themselves, "distinguished for the representativeness, their typicality, their 'will to ordinariness,' to be accepted, normalized, experienced as familiar."[17]

This familiarity allows the personality to work ideologically. In this particular MTV case, it enabled the VJs to call attention to specific videos, generate interest, and even influence video popularity without seeming overimposing. During the sampled week, hard-edged VJ Kennedy pointed out the poor reception of the newly released Smashing Pumpkins unit *Mellon Collie and the Infinite Sadness* on her alternative late-night show *Alternative Nation*. During the week Kennedy made further references to the album and lead video "Bullet with Butterfly Wings," inviting us to "call in and let us know what you think" and asking us, "is it really that bad?" The enthusiasm generated by Kennedy's remarks—coupled with the substantial

Table 2.2

MTV VJs, November 4–11, 1995 *

Regular VJs	Programs
Simon Rex	*Music Videos*
	Most Wanted
John Sencio	*Music Videos*
	Rude Awakening
	Top 20 Video Countdown
Bill Bellamy	*MTV Jams*
	Most Wanted Jams
	MTV Jams Countdown Weekend
Kennedy	*Music Videos*
	Alternative Nation
Erik Palladino	*Dreamtime*
Matt Pinfield	*120 Minutes*
Daisy Fuentes	*Top 20 Video Countdown*
Idalis	*Prime Time*

*The guest VJs that week included musician and nonmusician celebrities: Adam Oates, Apache Indian, Cindy Crawford, Chris Isaak, Coolio, Elastica, Genius, Jermaine Dupree, Killah Priest, Patra, Take That, Salt-N-Pepa, Shaquille O'Neal and Xscape.

airplay—culminated in its appearance on the *Top 20 Video Countdown* by the end of that week.

On MTV, programs often were linked not only with musical genres but also with VJ personalities. This additional connection deflected attention away from the mechanisms of power involved in selecting and orchestrating the video repertoire, implying instead that the video choices were not made by a corporation but by individuals we can see on the other side of the camera. "The effect of structuring television around personalities," Langer writes, "suggests that the world, first and foremost, is constructed through the actions of individuals behaving as free agents rather than by the complex relations among classes, institutions, and interest groups."[18] MTV's time-specific programming facilitated VJ/program/individual viewer associations; as our connection with the television personality strengthened, her power to influence the viewer from a seemingly "personal" space expanded and MTV's corporate-driven obligations became less conspicuous.

On MuchMusic, ten VJs were featured the week of the sample: eight were regular VJs and two were guests (the program *Rap City* was without a VJ. See table 2.3 for a list of VJs and shows).

Table 2.3

MuchMusic VJs, November 4–11, 1995 *

Regular VJs	Programs
Diego Fuentes	*Video Flow*
	R.S.V.P.
Sook-Yin Lee	*Video Flow*
	The Wedge
Mike Campbell	*MuchEast*
Terry David Mulligan	*MuchWest*
Natalie Richard	*Video Flow*
	French Kiss
Master "T"	*Da Mix*
Bill Welychka	*Video Flow*
	Cliptrip
	Intimate and Interactive Preview
	Daily R.S.V.P.
	MuchMusic Countdown (voice-over only)
Teresa Roncon	*Video Flow*
	Power 30
	Daily R.S.V.P.

*That week, MuchMusic featured Afrika Bambaataa and Soul Sonic Force as guest VJs.

It would be reasonable to assume that because MuchMusic included fewer VJs, a more stable and perhaps more predictable schedule would result. Unlike MTV, MuchMusic did not adjust programming to accommodate time zones. The station taped live for eight hours, then shuffled and repeated programs to make a twenty-four-hour cycle. All of this material was aired simultaneously across the country making nationwide time-specific shows impossible. If it was 6:00 A.M. in Newfoundland, the furthermost eastern point of Canada, it was only 1:30 A.M. in the West.

At least three significant differences between the two stations arise here. First, although MuchMusic aired the same shows at the same time each day, the VJ appearances were not always predictable. If I tuned in on Monday morning, Diego Fuentes was the video flow VJ; Tuesday morning it may have been Sook-Yin Lee. Their appearances on the video flow were not consistent. (On MTV it was always John Sencio who started my day with a cup of coffee in hand.) Second, that MuchMusic aired simultaneously across the country in different time zones resulted in different repertoires for its viewers. The videos a teenager was watching after school in Ontario were not what a British Columbian would see when she arrived home several hours later. Texans who watched MTV during their dinner hour, however, were watching the same repertoire as Californians sitting down several hours later. Finally, the farther Canadian viewers lived from the Toronto studio, the more they were temporally marginalized. A viewer in Vancouver might have been sitting in darkness while a MuchMusic VJ broadcasted live in daylight. MuchMusic's airing schedule, like the program listings, served to remind the viewer that he was one among many. MTV, meanwhile, insisted that the individual viewer's time zone overrode all others and that he was always the intended viewer.

And the "many" that constitute Canada's ethnic and racial mix were represented in more depth on MuchMusic by a diverse pool of regular VJs, including Natalie Richard (a Francophone), Sook-Yin Lee (of Chinese Canadian descent), Master "T" (of African Canadian descent), and Diego Fuentes, a Chilean Canadian. MuchMusic, in fact, drew attention to this diversity in their commercial promo for Diego Fuentes the week of the sample. Fuentes was introduced as the winner of a cross-Canada VJ search; in the commercial he stated: "I was born in Chile where it's hot / and moved to Canada, where it's not." To accentuate this geographical shift, he was shown sweating on sand for the first phrase and shivering in a sweater while holding hockey skates during the second (hockey is Canada's most popular sport). Here Fuentes clearly was identified (and celebrated) as part of Canada's Latin American immigrant population. That MuchMusic was filmed at streetfront level in Toronto is also significant. Toronto repeatedly has been identified by the United Nations as the "most multicultural" city in the world. The richly varied fans who crowded the studio or watched from outside were reflected daily by the lineup of diverse VJs. Conversely, on MTV, with the exception of Cuban American Daisy Fuentes who hosted one show that week, the station featured regularly scheduled VJs of either African or European descent.

In addition to scheduling differences and ethnicity, a further distinguishing feature between the VJs was their accessibility vis-à-vis their physical locations and their mode of address. MTV was recorded in a decontextualized studio setting; where it was filmed exactly was speculative for the viewing audience member. Moreover, the VJs (and guest celebrities) used teleprompters/cues, so that they did not appear to be reading the information, but simply reporting it. On MuchMusic, the VJs most often were shown reading information off handheld charts. In addition, the cameras were often moving in the "interactive" environment: MuchMusic employees were shown working in and around the streetfront set, while the VJ picked up information to be read to the home audience. The mechanical technology here was intentionally exposed.

These differences illustrate well Erving Goffman's notion of "front" and "back" regions, conceptual boundaries that can help differentiate the power relations between VJ and viewer on the two stations.[19] In this particular context, the front region included the VJs' performances on camera, whereas the back region was the "behind the scenes" activity. MTV made a clear separation between the preparation of information and its dissemination; MuchMusic, however, collapsed front and back regions, resulting in a different relationship between the viewer and the VJ. Joshua Meyerowitz has pointed out that hierarchical structures depend to different degrees on concealing or revealing back regions. Highly hierarchical roles usually conceal backstage preparation, rehearsals, and practice. The higher the individual's status, the more likely the backstage is denied.[20] Herein lies one of the significant hierarchical differences between the two stations. On MuchMusic, VJs appeared to be more like "us": they read prepared texts, sometimes misread texts, and apparently learned the information simultaneously with the viewer. On MTV, the VJs were "already knowing." This discrepancy between the VJs results in two distinct degrees of status. "The information possessed by very high status people," Meyerowitz argues, "must appear to be not only 'unknown,' but 'unknowable,' wherein hierarchical roles involve both mystery and 'mystification.'" He argues further, "The greater the ability to hide the time and effort needed to maintain a high status role . . . the greater one's seeming power and omnipotence."[21] Moreover, that these "all knowing" VJs were prerecorded in an unidentified setting further increased their power. As John Shepherd has argued, "the conceptualization of people as objects decontextualized from social relations implies the possibility for uncontested, unilateral control."[22] On MuchMusic, VJs were chosen, in part, because of their ability to represent a plurality of racial and ethnic backgrounds; their style of dissemination from visible locals reinforced their ordinariness, further enabling the viewers to read themselves into the role of the VJ.

Thus MuchMusic's VJs resembled their viewers more so than those on MTV. Their role was demystified and rendered common, preparing their way to function as the mediator between the viewer and the visiting celebrity. This emphasis on mediation illustrates another distinguishing feature between the two stations in their constructions of imagined communities: the role of the guest celebrities. Two primary stylistic differences separated the stations with regard to guest participation: live musical performances and the use of direct address. On MuchMusic, guests usually performed live (and live-to-air) in the studio.[23] The week of this sample MuchMusic featured live musical performances by Meatloaf, Melissa Etheridge, and others on programs like *Intimate and Interactive*, where audience members can

Alanis Morissette performing inside the MuchMusic studio environment *(Photo courtesy of MuchMusic)*

ask questions and talk with the performer, as well as within the general video flow. By extension, the fans also were shown within the studio setting, sometimes only inches away from the performer. The audience overflow who braved the weather outside on Queen Street, meanwhile, looked through huge windows for a glimpse of the celebrity—or, in many cases, the celebrity exited through these windows to interact with the fans outside.

The presence of the audience here is significant. As David Marshall has pointed out within the forum of television talk shows, the audience "constructs an atmosphere of an event that is particularized in time and place."[24] I would extend this argument to MuchMusic and suggest that the audience contributed to these moments of temporal specificity. Conversely, MTV did not feature live musical performances in the loft and no audience appeared. Guest stars like Coolio, Elastica, or Killah Priest even replaced regular VJs, whereas on MuchMusic, the VJ interviewed the celebrities while the audience posed questions. In every case the VJ was retained to mediate between the celebrity and us.

A further difference between the interactive styles of the guest stars on the two stations concerns the use of direct address. Direct address was discussed previously with regard to the interruption of household flow, but it also affects hierarchical structures among the viewer, the VJ, and the celebrity. The differentiation here between the two stations is straightforward.

Usher outside the MuchMusic environment on Queen Street, Toronto *(Photo courtesy of MuchMusic)*

Visiting celebrities on MTV looked directly at the camera; guests on MuchMusic, other than a quick glance, never did. As noted previously, Kurt Danziger argues that it is through direct address that the celebrity seems to be taking the viewer into account, of speaking directly to her. He continues: "appearing to reduce distance through intimacy the personality system operates to mask the gap between the powerful and the powerless, ensuring that the real unities of power, class, prestige and interest can continue relatively intact and unexamined."[25] That MTV celebrities talked to us directly blurred existing hierarchies and made our ascension from viewer to VJ to celebrity slightly more plausible, despite overwhelming odds to the contrary. The gap between the powerful and powerless is minimized as the star speaks directly to me, the individual viewer.

I would argue that the parallel to MTV's direct address was the appearance of the crowd on MuchMusic. The significant difference is that the celebrity on MTV spoke to the viewer. This direct address suggests that the distance between the celebrity and viewer could be overcome, thus evoking a form of American individualism. On MuchMusic, meanwhile, the star who addressed the VJ and/or performed for the crowd (and, by extension, for the television viewer), was speaking to *us,* that is, a Canadian collective. The distance between viewer and celebrity was not elided and the hierarchy from viewer to audience member to VJ to star—from the most powerless to the most powerful—may be argued as more realistic than that hierarchy depicted on MTV.

The Video Repertoires

That we were encouraged to imagine ourselves as part of a broader collective on MuchMusic differentiates the two stations. I support this argument by commenting briefly on two features of the actual video repertoires: variance of language and historical depth.

First, the stations reinforced the viewing population's uniformity or diversity through language. Of the 1,033 videos shown on MTV that week, only four video events were not in English: one French video, "69 Annee Erotique" featuring East Coast–based Luscious Jackson was aired four times that week. The languages from MuchMusic's video repertoire were more varied: 1,357 videos were in English, sixty-three in French (mostly on the show *French Kiss*), fourteen in Spanish, and seven in languages other than these three,(including, among others, Ukrainian and Punjabi). MuchMusic's repertoire simply contained more linguistic diversity than MTV's.

Second, the imagined communities were constructed differently vis-à-vis the historical depth of the video repertoires. MuchMusic's repertoire included a considerably greater number of older videos whereas MTV's was extremely current. As part of my analysis, individual videos were coded according to their "special video identifications." New videos on MTV were called "Buzz Clips"; on MuchMusic, they were labeled "Fresh New Vibes" or "New Power 30" videos. I then collapsed these labels and arrived at six categories (shown in table 2.4).

We see from table 2.4 that MTV was more aggressive in airing new videos than MuchMusic. MTV also informed the viewer when it had bought exclusive rights to a video (over other American stations), whereas MuchMusic didn't engage in this practice (owing to less direct competition). Each station had one featured video per week that totaled about the same number (thirty on MTV, twenty-eight on MuchMusic), and MuchMusic aired requested videos whereas MTV did not.[26] The most striking difference between the two is the discrepancy between the numbers in the final line of table 2.4, videos from the 1980s and very early 1990s: thirty-nine on

Table 2.4

MTV and MuchMusic's Special Video Identifications

	MTV	MuchMusic
New Videos	87	36
Exclusive Videos	24	0
Featured Videos	30	28
Requested Videos	0	26
Indie	0	4
Dated Videos	0	39

MuchMusic, none on MTV. It should be noted that MTV *did* show a few older videos, although they were not identified as such. These videos included a portion of Michael Jackson's 1983 "Billie Jean," and UB40's 1983 release "Red Red Wine" (which charted in the United States later in 1988). With only a few exceptions the vast majority of MTV's video repertoire was taken from the 1990s, predominantly from 1993 to 1995. On MuchMusic, meanwhile, a total of thirty-nine older videos were aired, including videos like Bon Jovi's "Runaway" (1984) and Cameo's "She's Strange" (1984).

MuchMusic was able to show a wider range of videos for two reasons: they showed more videos that week overall (1,457 to MTV's 1,033) and they used a slower rotation. That means that the top artists were shown more frequently on MTV than they were on MuchMusic. In fact, the top twelve artists on MTV were featured in 35.4 percent of all the videos shown. The top twelve artists on MuchMusic accounted for 20.1 percent of their repertoire. Overall, an expanded repertoire was possible because of MuchMusic's effort to slow the rotation and show more videos by a wider range of artists.

Of course, MuchMusic might be expected to feature an expanded repertoire because of Canadian content regulations determined by the CRTC; in addition, because it has less network competition, it can target a wider demographic market. Its primary competitors in 1995 were country music stations and video programs shown on Black Entertainment Television. MTV, in addition to these stations, also competed with VH1, a co-owned station with an older 25 to 40–year-old target demographic, The Box, Much USA, Z Music Television (a Nashville-based Christian video network), among others. With this group of competing stations, MTV might have been expected to narrow their playlist to appeal to the younger 12 to 24–year-old demographic. Yet, consider how much of the video market was actually controlled by MTV: in 1993 they were 57.4 million subscribers strong in the United States. That same year, VH1 had 47.2 million viewers.[27] Targeting the 25 to 40-year-old group proved difficult for VH1; in fact, ratings had been so low that Viacom (owner of MTV and VH1) grappled with selling the two stations together as a either a package or not at all, knowing that operators couldn't afford to lose MTV.[28] In short, MTV simply had the stranglehold on the U.S. market for all demographics in 1995. I point this out simply because one might not surmise MTV's power from its limited playlist. Like the programming flow discussed earlier, the limited video repertoire reinforced the perception of a relatively narrow range of viewers.

Station Commercials

Differences in station commercials also contributed to distinctive imagined communities on either side of the border. During the twelve-hour sample, MTV featured a total of five station commercials, which can be further divided into two subgroups. The first included commercials that attempted to depict MTV in a lighthearted, playful, even irresponsible light. In one commercial, American painter Bob Ross paints a gentle outdoor landscape, commenting on his process as he adds scenery and wildlife. (Ross was famous for his highly rated television show, *The Joy of Painting*, in which he would instruct viewers how to paint "happy little clouds" and "happy little trees.") By the commercial's end, the artwork is revealed to be in the shape of the MTV logo. Ross comments: "MTV. It's all just fluffy white clouds." MTV was presented humorously through Ross, an unthreatening spokesperson.

Juxtaposed with this style is another, more purposeful one, intended to align the station specifically with the young viewing audience. Several different commercials that aired that week evidence this style. In one, MTV President Gwendolyn VanDeerlin is shown in a black dress, hair partially down, lying comfortably (and seductively) on a sofa. The accompanying music is in a minor mode with fast, suspenseful arpeggiation in the upper keyboard register:

Hi, I'm Gwendolyn VanDeerlin, President of MTV. As you know, MTV has always been against censorship, but the growing number of multiple-career MTV families has made parental supervision more difficult *(camera pans the room, a piece of paper and glasses are shown on furniture, reminding the viewer of her professional status)*. That's why we recommend the MTV chip *(chip is shown, held in hand)*. This simple device inserted in your TV set will allow you to limit the amount of time your parents watch MTV *(image of adult in front of television with remote in hand)*. Don't let the government control what your parents can watch. That's your job. *(Male dub-over voice and text shown on screen: "MTV: It's a right and a responsibility.")*

In addition to its satirically humorous content (a common feature of MTV commercials), this commercial also functions in establishing at least four distinct groups: the parents, the viewers, MTV (aligned with the viewers), and the government, which oversees all. In this instance, the viewers are homogenized and treated as a single unity that must band together to "save" their parents and protect themselves from the government's dangerous directives.

MuchMusic's commercials, meanwhile, tended to be more playful, without identifying collectivities. In "The Mime" commercial, for instance, a mime unsuccessfully performs a series of movements, including the moonwalk and the robot; he is hit with a brick at the end as "MuchMusic" and "Express Yourself" are written across the screen. MuchMusic's commercials, while arguably subversive, were extremely playful and self-identified as "low-budget"; they refused to take any sort of overt stance on any topic. Unlike the MTV commercials that delineated the viewing audience by making distinctions among them, their parents, and the government, MuchMusic tended to include humor, but did not strive for shared cohesiveness of viewing subgroups.

Time, Space, and Media Biases

This rather detailed analysis has attempted to delineate how the extra-musical parameters on MuchMusic reinforced the perception of a wide-ranging audience. This perception extended from their programming on the half-hour level, to the presence of the studio audience and the VJs who represent Canada's multiethnic plurality, to the twelve-year historical depth of the video repertoire. I would argue that through these initiatives, Much-Music evoked and reinforced discursively produced Canadian narratives of plurality and collectivity. Compare this with MTV, where programming did not delineate musical preferences so sharply, but where the individual, rather than the collective, was always prioritized. VJs and guests spoke to the individual viewer while they announced artists and videos with either a cup of coffee in the morning or surrounded by candles at night. This was where the video repertoire was always presented as current, and where the commercials identified us as the youth (even if only satirically) who should be wary of authority figures.

The sum of these differences can be more broadly identified by their media biases, which, in turn, indicate additional national inflections. For insight into these partialities, I borrow from the work of communications theorist and historian Harold Innis.[29] In *The Bias of Communication*, Innis details how Western communications media privilege space over time. Kim Sawchuck summarizes that "[Innis's] concepts of space and time articulated a theory of power for both realms: hierarchical (temporal . . . based in the oral tradition) and decentralized (spatial . . . based on the eye)."[30] In other words, time-biased media emphasize interpersonal, short-distance communication; space-biased media (which include print media, telegraphs, and today's communication technologies such as computers and satellites) facilitate the control and quick dissemination of information over far-reaching geographical spaces. Easily replaceable and hypercurrent, these technologies accentuate what Innis calls "the modern obsession with present-mindedness,"[31] while their users propagate the myth that newer is not only better, it is necessary.

When MTV's 1995 programming is considered within a space and time model, their bias is clear. Their determination to interrupt household flow illustrated their concern with the visual realm; the ear, secondary to the eye, was used between the videos as a mechanism to direct the viewer back to the visual stimuli. MTV further biased space in its rapid dissemination of videos, its currency, and its adaptability through its own timelessness (separate from that of the viewer), its placelessness, and its erasure of collective cultural history. As a result, MTV was extremely mobile. As their slogan proudly asserted: "MTV: Coming to you wherever you are."[32]

As Jody Berland puts it, the sacrifices for space bias are significant:

The American empire's predilection for conquering space through media . . . is expressed in its extension of the modernizing, visualizing, and rationalizing space-bias of paper and print . . . obliterating media appropriate to memory, tradition, spirituality, dialogue: all aspects of oral culture that have been appropriated and transformed through the production of technological space.[33]

A time-biased medium, as Berland points out, facilitates a sense of history and memory, thus enabling the individual to situate herself within that history. While MuchMusic obviously could not operate exclusively as a time-biased medium, an oral emphasis was clearly injected into its style and content. This emphasis was particularly true when it attempted to make explicit the hierarchical positions among the celebrity, VJ, and viewer by retaining the VJ to speak to the celebrity on behalf of, and alongside, the viewing audience (MTV elided these unequal positions through such techniques as direct address and the absence of an audience). On MuchMusic's live performance shows, such as *Intimate and Interactive,* orality was brought into clear focus as audience members were invited to ask questions of the celebrity by phone, e-mail, fax, or in the form of face-to-face dialogue within the studio. As Innis notes, "the oral tradition involves personal contact and a consideration of the feelings of others"[34]—precisely what MuchMusic attempted to capture in its programming through emotionally intense and engaging personal discussion. When viewed alongside its historically broader video playlist and its explicit temporal and geographical specificity within downtown Toronto, MuchMusic clearly privileged the hierarchical time-biased model articulated by Innis a half-century ago.

While both stations have changed stylistically since 1995, change has been particularly dramatic at MTV: after the launching of MTV2, a station dedicated primarily to airing music videos, MTV continued to diversify its programming beyond the video repertoire. As a result, MTV now airs considerably more (often syndicated) programs at the half-hour level, while MTV2 featured longer video segments. Moreover, the addition of more recent programs to MTV's lineup suggests that it has been moving toward MuchMusic's time-biased model. MTV's program *Total Request Live* (TRL) is a case in point. I do not suggest that *TRL* has adopted MuchMusic's format verbatim: the aired videos are abridged while e-mailed viewer messages are scrolled across the bottom of the screen; all of this is intercut with enthusiastic "live" messages from audience members who momentarily displace the videos both visually and sonically. It could be argued, then, that while some of MTV's programming has moved toward MuchMusic's model (available to American viewers via MuchUSA), the station has developed—in relation to the audience—unique and effective strategies to draw our attention back to the television screen itself, thus sustaining their high level of televisual flow.

Unlike viewers who tuned into MTV, MuchMusic's 1995 Canadian audience members—like the viewers who tune in today—frequently were reminded that the videos they enjoyed represented only a fragment of a wide range of musical styles, and that their generation was but one of many that cross musical tastes, linguistic boundaries, and multiple time zones. By reinforcing discursively produced narratives of cultural diversity and social collectivity, MuchMusic inflected MTV's highly successful format to create new, uniquely *Canadian* imagined communities, where individuals were invited to participate in a collective celebration of popular music and musical life in Canada.

CHAPTER THREE

"Simple Economics"
Images of Gender and Nationality

[In the 1950s] teenage girls did participate in the new public sphere afforded by the growth of the leisure industries, but they could consume also at home, upstairs in their bedrooms. . . . [B]oys tended to have a more participative and a more technically-informed relationship with pop, where girls in contrast became fans and readers of pop-influenced love comics.
—Angela McRobbie and Jenny Garber, "Girls and Subcultures"

Girls' relationships to music clearly have changed since McRobbie and Garber first published this passage in 1978. More young women now perform as instrumentalists in after-school garage bands and each summer thousands of them attend rock camps across North America. Female DJs also are emerging on the club scene with energy and fervor, learning how to mix beats and set up equipment, breaking through the vinyl ceiling. From these more recent practices it is clear that while girls still spend time consuming and producing music from behind closed bedroom doors, they also enjoy those activities in more public spaces. I do not mean to suggest that women historically have not wanted to participate more openly; overt and covert processes of exclusion kept them at bay, especially when it came to historically male-dominated instruments (the electric guitar) and genres (especially rock).[1] While trends have changed and opportunities for females to be active participants and consumers of popular music have increased, I shall argue here that women's musical performances are still bounded by their gender, as they are by their race and nationality. Today, however, these women are pushing up against newer, shinier, technologically enhanced—and therefore often less visible—glass ceilings.

Historically, instrumentation and instrumental virtuosity have been associated with male musical performance practices. Here I use MTV's and MuchMusic's video repertoires to explore how women carve out such social spaces by means of acoustic versus electric instrumental musical performance, and how women's instrumental participation is similar and different on the two stations. For instance, I argue that during the sample MTV and MuchMusic aired videos that presented a coherent subgroup of female Euro-American instrumentalists who were markedly different from their Euro-Canadian counterparts and that these patterns reinforced existing national narratives. I do not suggest that the stations' programming directors chose to air videos based on women's instrumentation in order to produce or reinforce these narratives. Videos are entered into and played in rotation based on a number of factors, including the release of new videos, Canadian content quotas, and viewer requests, among other factors. Further, as noted previously, MuchMusic was expected to air more Canadian-made videos, and this stipulation resulted in a repertoire different from MTV's. Despite their different repertoires, however, there was a striking parallel between the videos aired on both stations: they often reinforced similar representational patterns, and in turn, co-participated in what it meant to be a "Canadian" or an "American."

I then consider Canadian and American women's celebrity status as it is constructed within the performance contexts. "Live" performances have been widely viewed within video scholarship as a critical marketing tool.[2] I shall also argue here for their ideological importance: artists' personas are constructed, in part, relative to the symbolic power of the live concert context and through other visible interactions with the audience. American performers were portrayed more consistently as surrounded by adoring fans, while Canadian artists lacked that social validation, producing ideological effects that extend beyond the artists to perceptions of the nations as a whole. Here I examine the intersection of gender, race, and nationality within the highly integral musical performance axis of both stations' video repertoires, the differences and similarities between the two stations in this regard, and, most important, the social significances stemming from these differences.

Gender/Instrumentation/Nation

Female rock music instrumentalists have always been far less common than female vocalists. According to McRobbie and Garber, young girls during the 1970s preferred to sing in their bedrooms, idolizing their favorite performers rather than engage in technologically enhanced performances. Accordingly, girls (and subsequently, women) tended to excel at vocal rather than instrumental performance. Mavis Bayton has forwarded explanations for the relatively few female electric guitar performers.

Among the major obstacles she identifies are: the discourse surrounding electric guitars in music magazines ("masculinized" and alienating); that girls are forced to break with a "feminine" tradition by cutting their nails; the lack of access to transport and equipment necessary for rehearsal and performances; and that women are conditioned to regard electronic technology as intimidating.

My interest here is not to explore why women electric guitarists have been so rare. Instead, I examine (a) the extent to which, in 1995, women appeared as instrumentalists on MTV and MuchMusic, (b) how instrumental representations differed on the two stations, and (c) possible influences upon women's choice of instrumentation. Rather than focus on female electric guitar players exclusively, I shall consider representations of all female instrumentalists within the video repertoires, and return to the guitar players later. This wide-ranging exploration is premised on the assumptions that (1) women instrumentalists possess significant symbolic power (even female instrumentalists who appear in the background have a significant influence on youth, especially aspiring female musicians in the viewing audience seeking out role models); and (2) if differing representational patterns exist, notions of female sexuality/agency/identity may also contrast.

I do not suggest that any artist shown performing an instrument is equal in stature to the next. Performers are highly differentiated and ascribed varying degrees of power according to many factors, especially gender. As Jody Berland has noted, when a man is shown playing a guitar "the camera makes love to his fingers, his face and his body's bounce. If she is a woman, it is, in the dominant code, her mouth and the gestures of her neck."[3] Here, Berland articulates the extent to which camera angles and editing techniques are determined by gender, relegating women, not surprisingly, to sexualized positions at the expense of their musicianship.

Perhaps the clearest example of women's hypersexualization that results in a lack of instrumental credibility in a music video is Robert Palmer's 1986 "Addicted to Love" (which, ironically, won a Grammy for Best Male Rock Performance in 1987).[4] Excellent descriptions of this video have already been undertaken;[5] nonetheless I would like to highlight a few points here that minimize women's instrumental authority. In this video, women dressed as mannequins play instruments but do not look at them, nor do they relate emotionally to the music. Instead, the "band" of identical brunettes stare straight ahead while moving their bodies mechanically to the beat. The video includes close-up shots of hands playing guitars, but never do these shots reveal the performer and their hands in the same frame. This suggests that these are not in fact the performers' hands (a male performer would be shown at least from the waist up to reveal how he is connecting to the instrument as an extension of his body). Moreover, Palmer stands in front of the drummer and never do we see a full-on shot of her playing. While it is easier to fake a performance on a guitar (where the guitar part is composed exclusively of chords), it is more difficult to fake a believable performance on a drum kit. Palmer's strategic positioning only confirms what we already know: it is totally implausible that these women are the instrumentalists on the original recording. And this is presented unabashedly in the video.

Unlike Palmer's "Addicted to Love," all of the videos from the current sample that include women instrumentalists depict them in a manner that is not mocking; rather, the depictions contribute a sense of authenticity and commitment to the music. From D'arcy Wretzky's loud and edgy bass guitar performance on the Smashing Pumpkins' "Bullet With Butterfly Wings" to Lisa Loeb's more moderate acoustic guitar playing on "Do You Sleep?" women are shown as professional instrumentalists, sometimes in addition to their roles as vocalists. This statement, of course should be qualified: varying editing techniques will depict some performers as more accomplished, committed, and believable than others. Viewers also will bring to the videos their own interpretive skills, expectations, biases, and the history of the artist as they watch these women perform. Nonetheless, the videos from this sample illustrate the important strides women took in instrumental performance since Palmer's 1986 hyper-femme imposters.

I begin my consideration of women and instrumental performance by examining the MTV repertoire. The week of the sample, MTV featured sixteen different videos that included female instrumentalists (identified in table 3.1). These sixteen videos were repeated during the week for a total of 137 airings. The most frequently aired five videos were the Smashing Pumpkins' "Bullet with Butterfly Wings" (24 of the 137 airings), Morissette's "Hand In My Pocket" (19 airings), Etheridge's "Your Little Secret" (18), Loeb's "Do You Sleep?" (17) and the Toadies' "Possum Kingdom" (16). In total, these five videos constituted 68.6 percent of all videos featuring female instrumentalists; the other nine videos made up the remaining 31.4 percent.

Meanwhile, MuchMusic aired twenty-nine different videos featuring female instrumentalists; the names of the videos and artists are listed in table 3.2. These videos combined were aired 140 times. Those most frequently aired were (once again) Smashing Pumpkins' "Bullet with Butterfly Wings" (22 airings), Morissette's "Hand In My Pocket" (21), Bass is Base's "Diamond Dreams" (17), Weeping Tile's "U.F.O. Rosie" (11), and

Table 3.1

MTV Videos Featuring Female Instrumentalists

Video	Instrumentalist (instrument)
"Cannonball"	The Breeders (electric guitar)
"Come"	Cimarron (electric guitar)
"Your Little Secret"	Melissa Etheridge (electric guitar)
"Doll Parts"	Hole (electric guitar, electric bass, and drums)
"Violet"	Hole (electric guitar, electric bass, and drums)
"Do You Sleep?"	Lisa Loeb (acoustic guitar)
"Hand In My Pocket"	Alanis Morissette (harmonica)
"Walk This World"	Heather Nova (acoustic guitar)
"Hard Times"	Queen Latifah (piano)
"Friends of P"	The Rentals (electric keyboard)
"Push It"	Salt-N-Pepa (turntable)
"Bullet With Butterfly Wings"	Smashing Pumpkins (electric bass)
"Disarm"	Smashing Pumpkins (electric bass)
"Rocket"	Smashing Pumpkins (electric bass)
"Possum Kingdom"	Toadies (electric guitar)
"More Human than Human"	White Zombie (electric bass)

Lisa Loeb's "Do You Sleep?" (10), constituting 57.8 percent of the overall percentage of videos featuring female instrumentalists.

A quick scan of these two lists reveals several glaring discrepancies between the two stations' repertoires. First, MuchMusic aired close to twice the number of different videos featuring female instrumentalists (twenty-nine to sixteen). This difference is partly explained by the obligation of MuchMusic to meet Canadian content quotas. Even so, it would have been entirely possible for the station to air fewer videos by promising up-and-coming and established Canadian musicians (as MTV did for American artists). The choice to air a wider range of artists, then, was not externally mandated. Second, because MTV occasionally aired more than one video by a single group, only thirteen distinct women/groups of women were shown as instrumentalists on that station. While airing more videos featuring fewer artists limited the range of female instrumentalists, the appearance of two different videos featuring the same band on MTV contributed to their construction as a "successful" group. More than just a "one video band," groups like Hole and Smashing Pumpkins could be read by the viewer as more popular/significant than their peers (they have at least two different videos out there, could there be more?). The heavier rotation of these groups, then, contributed to their heightened celebrity

Table 3.2

MuchMusic Videos Featuring Female Instrumentalists

Video	Instrumentalist (instrument)
"Diamond Dreams"	Bass is Base (electric keyboard)
"Super-Connected"	Belly (electric guitar and electric bass)
"Shocker in the Gloomroom"	The Breeders (electric guitar)
"Wild Country"	Robert Burton and the Strange (electric bass)
"Ace of Spades"	Coal (electric guitar)
"Bring Me Some Water"	Melissa Etheridge (acoustic guitar)
"Our Lips are Sealed"	Fun Boy Three (electric bass, electric guitar, electric keyboard, drums, percussion, and cello)
"Dizzy"	Green Apple Quickstep (electric bass)
"What a Life"	Juliana Hatfield (electric guitar)
"Miss World"	Hole (electric guitar, electric bass, and drums)
"Andres"	L7 (electric guitar and drums)
"Do You Sleep?"	Lisa Loeb (acoustic guitar)
"Prends bien garde"	Julie Masse (electric keyboard)
"Fade into You"	Mazzy Star (percussion)
"I Will Remember You"	Sarah McLaughlin (piano)
"I Wish"	The Misunderstood (electric keyboard)
"Hand In My Pocket"	Alanis Morissette (harmonica)
"Kashmir"	The Ordinaires (electric guitar and violin)
"Tout pour toi"	Genevieve Paris (acoustic guitar)
'Rock Steady"	Bonnie Raitt (electric guitar)
"Pense à moi"	Francine Raymond (acoustic guitar)
"Ecstasy"	Rusted Root (percussion)
"Bullet With Butterfly Wings"	Smashing Pumpkins (electric bass)
"Kool Thing"	Sonic Youth (electric bass)
"And if Venice Were Sinking"	Spirit of the West (accordion)
"Tragic Flaw"	Suzanne Little (acoustic guitar)
"My Name is Luka"	Suzanne Vega (acoustic guitar)
"Upfront with You"	Universal Honey (electric guitar)
"U.F.O. Rosie"	Weeping Tile (electric guitar and electric bass)

status. Conversely, on MuchMusic, each group was featured in only one video thus limiting this mode of celebrity construction, resulting in a wider range of twenty-nine different artists/groups of artists.

When the airing frequency of these videos is calculated, more differences ensue. The top five videos on MuchMusic added up to 57.8 percent of the female instrumentalist repertoire, slightly less than 68.6 percent on MTV, thus allowing for more airtime for the other twenty-four artists. Although MuchMusic did not show as many videos featuring female performers proportionally (140 of MuchMusic's total 1,457 aired is proportionally fewer than 137 of MTV's 1,033), their wider range of videos means that female instrumentalists likely would have been seen by viewers spanning a variety of musical tastes (from fans of Bonnie Raitt to Hole to Francine Raymond). These viewers were predominantly limited, however, to fans of white performers. With few exceptions, all of these instrumentalists were Caucasians of European descent.

Making interpretive distinctions between MuchMusic's wide range of female instrumentalists versus MTV's more limited playlist based on the information thus far would be invalid because we cannot distinguish between those videos aired repeatedly versus those aired only once. On which instruments then did women perform most often on MTV and MuchMusic? Was there a correlation between the stations and women performing acoustic or electric guitars, keyboards, or even harmonicas? Table 3.3 indicates on which instruments women played on both stations.

Women on MTV played electric guitar and bass most frequently, followed by the electric keyboard. Acoustic instrumental performances were less prevalent. That electric instruments—particularly the guitar and bass—vastly outnumbered the other acoustic instruments more traditionally performed by women (piano or auxiliary percussion, such as cowbell or the tambourine), or the acoustic guitar (from the folk singer–songwriter tradition) is significant as women traditionally have been discouraged from electrified musical production. Women on MuchMusic, meanwhile, played the electric bass most often, followed by the electric guitar and the keyboard. Acoustic instrumental performance was more frequent on MuchMusic than on MTV with more women performing on acoustic guitar, drums, percussion, accordion, and violin.

One could argue that women on MuchMusic were less visible than women on MTV because they played the electric bass more often than the electric guitar; the higher number of women playing acoustic instruments on MuchMusic only serves to corroborate this assertion. This argument leads us to more problematic questions. Should we hold up electric instrumental performance as a sign of "progress" and "equality" against which other forms of instrumental performance should be compared? Should women necessarily strive to play electric guitar with the same frequency as men? According to Mavis Bayton, yes:

I look forward to the day when there will be as many women playing electric guitar in bands as men. . . . If as many women played [electric] guitar as men . . . [p]laying rock would no longer denote masculinity. In a non-sexist world half of all electric guitarists would be women and gender would be no more relevant to playing than eye colour or height is today.[6]

Table 3.3

MTV and MuchMusic: Instruments Performed by Female Artists

MTV	Percent of total number played by female artists*	MuchMusic	Percent of total number played by female artists**
Electric Guitar	29.1%	Electric Guitar	21.8%
Electric Bass	24.1%	Electric Bass	27.6%
Electric Keyboard	21.3%	Electric Keyboard	16.7%
Harmonica	13.5%	Harmonica	13.5%
Acoustic Guitar	7.8%	Acoustic Guitar	9.0%
Drum kit	1.4%	Drum kit	3.2 %
Auxiliary percussion	0.0%	Auxiliary percussion	4.5%
Piano	2.8%	Piano	1.3%
Accordion	0.0%	Accordion	1.9%
Violin	0.0%	Violin	0.6%

*(N = 137, where N = number of videos)
**(N = 140)

Bayton makes several assertions here that are problematic. First, she argues that if women equaled the number of men playing electric guitar, playing rock "would no longer denote masculinity." What she overlooks in her analysis is the possibility that masculinity may be *reinscribed* by women within the musical performance context, intentionally or not, as a means of musical survival. Indeed, the electric guitar has for so long been defined as a male instrument that, as Steve Waksman points out, even before the guitarist plays, "the instrument carries certain associations that are inscribed onto the body of the performer."[7] For women to separate the guitar from the associations of the male body and redefine the relationship among masculinity, femininity, and rock, then, is a significant undertaking. Indeed, it may be impossible for rock music ever to lose its gendered associations: according to Rob Walser, rock "is intelligible only in its historical and discursive contexts"; only through antisexist performances that consciously disrupt rock's gender representations may change be possible.[8] More women participants, then, do not *necessarily* result in a less sexist subculture; rather, change depends upon how these women perform the instrument within this genre.

Second, Bayton awaits with anticipation when as many women will play electric guitar as men; she suggests that more women on electric guitar signifies access and a "better" situation for women. According to Bayton's thesis, more women would further the project of gender equality; a second hypothesis, however, one stemming from research into women's relationships with computer technologies, might suggest otherwise. Sherry Turkle has argued that women's socialization into technology is complex, and its seemingly positive trajectory—the more women who engage in technology the better—has not been established. Turkle points out that women historically have been viewed as phobic of machines and/or lacking in ability. More accurately, she argues, it is computer culture, with traditions of competition and violence that has been unappealing for women.[9] A number of factors make this subculture particularly uninviting. First, during adolescence, the (usually male) enthusiast finds in computers a sort of "safe" relationship; it becomes a "partner" without any possibility of rejection or actual human intimacy. Women, however, are less likely to insulate themselves within such formal systems and artificial worlds to escape societal anxieties.[10] Second, within computer subcultures, hacking is associated with a severe sense of risk taking. Hackers talk about living "on the edge," of pushing their bodies and minds beyond what even they thought possible. Taking risks, as Turkle points out, is something girls find difficult because the socialization of young women to be "good students" necessitates a certain stability and predictability rather than uncertainty.[11] Third, because the computer is the interface between the programmer and a formal system, it is susceptible to anthropomorphism. As she states, "being a woman is opposed to a compelling relationship with a thing that shuts people out."[12] Turkle does not advocate here that what is needed is more women working with computers. Instead, she questions whether women's vehemence will shift when they can "experience it as material which allows highly differentiated styles of mastery and personalizes the world of formal systems for men and women alike."[13]

Admittedly, both the subculture and technology that Turkle analyzes here differ somewhat from those of the electric guitar. Yet, important parallels can be drawn. First, like the practice found within computer subcultures, many boys tend to become more actively involved in creating bands and developing relationships with their instruments (particularly the electric guitar) during adolescence, a reaction partly due to increased societal pressures whereby the instrument becomes a "safe" relationship. Close relationships between male guitarists and their electric guitars have been well documented. B. B. King, for instance, has owned a series of guitars, each of which, since 1949, he lovingly has called "Lucille." King has described these guitars fondly, sometimes as a personal savior: "she's taken me a long way . . . she's kept me alive, being able to eat."[14] At another point on the spectrum, Jimi Hendrix was notorious for being assertive and occasionally violent with his guitars on stage, simulating sex by swiveling his hips and rubbing up against them, then setting them on fire or smashing them against his amplifiers. (Such public sexual simulation with a guitar, of course, is available only to men; if women were to be intimate with a guitar on stage they likely would evoke same-sex desire—still an unmarketable commodity within the popular music industry.[15])

Second, electric guitar and computer subcultures share a level of commitment to individual technical mastery and control; this learning time is particularly true of the rock lead guitarist. The time necessary to "hack" and take risks is crucial to any performer's life (not just the guitar player's). Within the context of exposed, lead guitar playing in rock music, risk taking is particularly foregrounded at the level of technique, improvisation, and technological innovation. Only through "hacking" can a lead guitarist make mistakes, recover, and excel at the craft.

These are but a few of the parallels between the rock guitarist and computer hacker subculture. It's possible, then, that some women choose not to perform the electric guitar not (only) because of the overt sexism (evident in many instrumental subcultures), but because the electric guitar subculture would necessitate cutting off a psychosocial component that would be unhealthy. If this is true, we should address how the guitar could be written for, performed, designed, and taught so as to better serve both men and women rather than lament the underrepresentation of women playing guitar.

This underrepresentation of women guitarists, unfortunately, is perpetuated on a daily basis in popular music magazines. In 1993, for instance, *Rolling Stone* magazine published a list of the one hundred greatest guitar players and only two women made the cut: Joni Mitchell and Joan Jett.[16] Moreover, as David Segal points out, surprisingly there was little backlash to the gender imbalance on this list.[17] And, while the numbers of female guitarists in rock bands remains dismally low and these women fairly invisible, more women have been active as guitarists in indie pop/punk bands. From Kathleen Hanna (Bikini Kill), to Kat Bjelland (Babes in Toyland) to Kelley Deal (The Breeders), the numbers of women playing guitar have been increasing—although distinctions are made between lead rock and punk guitar playing, the former of which is often more technical, complex, and celebrated than the latter. So while there has been an increase in successful women guitarists in more alternative musics, they have been kept away from the cultural capital enjoyed by rock guitarists.

Turkle's analysis of gender differences in relation to computer technology, admittedly, is restrictive, and we have seen within musical realms how females have begun to make important strides. From punk and indie pop guitarists to female DJs to young girls in computer-music composition classes, the gender imbalance is shifting. Still, we continue to have an uneven representation of women on certain instruments and in particular genres and, it is important to note, these female-dominated expressions often are not afforded the credibility that is given to more male-dominated genres and instruments, including rock and especially the lead guitar.[18]

Returning to Bayton's criteria for evaluating gender equality vis-à-vis the electric guitar, it is possible that a reader would be impressed with the female performers on MTV because of the higher number of electric guitarists. This same reader would view MuchMusic as less "progressive" because it featured more women playing traditional acoustic instruments. But it also is possible to read this scenario differently, to interpret women's musical performances of nonelectrified instruments (violin, percussion, accordion) on MuchMusic as valid (and healthy) expressions of creativity rather than as a shortcoming. I do not intend to suggest here that women should or should not play electric guitar. Instead, I only challenge the notion that women's participation within the electric guitar subculture is *necessarily* a progressive and desirable route.

Another pattern overshadowed by the attention paid to the electric guitar subculture but that warrants consideration here is the number of women performing electric bass from the current sample (24.1 percent on MTV and 27.6 percent on MuchMusic). In 1990 Bayton noted a paucity of women on electric bass,[19] yet in this sample taken five years later it was the most frequently played instrument by women on MuchMusic and second only to the electric guitar on MTV. Rather than interpreting these data as women's attempts to play in bands while avoiding the technical mastery of lead guitarists, I wonder if this is a means for women both to participate in the electric guitar subculture, and *not* participate. One could read women's interest in playing the bass as a strategy to supply the ensemble's "glue" without appearing as the primary figure. This position may appeal to some women as a comfortable middleground, providing the opportunity to perform without the psychosocial burden that accompanies playing lead electric rock guitar (and this may also apply to the indie pop/punk guitarists described above).[20]

As evidenced here, then, women on MuchMusic performed a wider range of instruments, including more acoustic instruments, and crossed more musical genres in these musical performances than did women on MTV. Despite the stations' differences, however, there exists one important similarity. Three of the top five videos/artists overlapped on the two stations (the Smashing Pumpkins, Alanis Morissette, and Lisa Loeb) while the remaining two videos/artists did not. On MTV these two videos featured American performers Melissa Etheridge and the Toadies, while on MuchMusic they were Canadian bands Bass is Base and Weeping Tile.

These data indicate a pattern linking nationality with types of instrumental performance: MTV's and MuchMusic's video repertoires showcase more American women and Canadian women respectively. Table 3.4 outlines the data on female instrumentalists and nationality, by station.

The week of the sample MTV overwhelmingly featured American female instrumentalists. Alanis Morissette's "Hand in My Pocket" was the only video featuring a female Canadian-born instrumentalist aired that week on the station. Two videos featuring artists of explicitly "multiple" nationalities were Heather Nova's "Walk this World" and Hole's "Violet" and "Doll Parts."[21] The other twelve videos featured American artists exclusively. What these data indicate, then, is the frequency with which American instrumentalists were aired on MTV that week and how non-American women could have primarily been viewed as vocalists (again, with Morissette as the one exception). MuchMusic, meanwhile, aired only one video featuring artists of multiple nationalities ("Rock Steady" featuring Bonnie Raitt and Bryan Adams, an American and a Canadian) and one British video (Fun Boy's "Our Lips are Sealed.") The remainder of the videos that featured female instrumentalists was fairly evenly divided between Americans and Canadians, resulting in a considerably more balanced North American picture than that presented on MTV.

What these data do not tell us is which instruments these women performed most often and whether there was a correlation between Canadian and American women and electric or acoustic instrumental production. Sarah McLaughlin, for instance, might sound more "Canadian" because of her acoustic piano performance while The Breeders were decoded as more "American" because of their electric and amplified sound. Table 3.5 provides a breakdown by American and Canadian nationalities according to bass guitar, electric guitar, and instruments other than these two on MuchMusic (for instance, 69.8 percent of the time women were shown playing bass guitar on MTV, they were American performers).[22]

Table 3.4

MTV and MuchMusic: Appearance of Female Instrumentalists, by Nationality

MTV: Female Instrumentalists*		MuchMusic: Female Instrumentalists**	
American	76.6%	American	47.1%
Canadian	13.9%	Canadian	50.1%
Multiple	9.5%	Multiple	2.1%
British	0.0%	British	0.7%

*(N = 137)
**(N = 140)

Table 3.5

MuchMusic: Nationality of Individual Female Instrumentalists

Bass guitar			
American Women*	69.8%	Canadian Women**	25.6%
Electric guitar			
American Women	58.8%	Canadian Women	35.3%
Instruments other than electric guitar and electric bass			
American Women	26.6%	Canadian Women	70.9%

*(*N* = 66)
**(*N* = 70)

American women, then, were considerably more likely to be shown playing electric bass and electric guitar than Canadian women. Conversely, Canadians were depicted more often playing electric keyboard and acoustic instruments than their American counterparts. On MTV, a similar pattern was evidenced (see table 3.6).

Only three non-American women were shown as instrumentalists on MTV: Alanis Morissette on harmonica ("Hand In My Pocket"), Heather Nova (identified as having multiple nationalities) on acoustic guitar in "Walk this World" and Melissa Auf Der Maur (former electric bass player for Hole). The foreigners on MTV, then, were largely *acoustic* instrumentalists,[23] while American women performed both acoustic and electric instruments and were shown to have exclusive access to amplified, electric instruments.

That women from abroad were rarely depicted as instrumentalists on MTV itself is noteworthy. That they were not so electronically amplified as American women further contributes to MTV viewers' possible decoding of foreign women. The correlation here between American women and technology is significant. As Paul Théberge has argued, within the realm of musical performance it has become a social imperative to own new technologies. Technological innovation is not only a response to musicians' needs, but a force with which musicians must contend, driving technological obsolescence to become "both the rule and the rationale for increased consumption."[24] The correlation between technology, currency, and "Americanness," therefore, becomes visible against the backdrop of foreign acoustic female artists who perform in musical genres that are not so electrified (American band Hole playing alterative music versus Canadian Sarah McLaughlin performing pop). Technological imagery also intersects here with popular notions of star construction insofar as popular celebrities (particularly within the American music and film industries) are viewed as

Table 3.6

MTV: Nationality of Individual Female Instrumentalists

Bass guitar

American Women* 93.8%   Canadian Women** 6.2%

Electric guitar

American Women 100%   Canadian Women 0%

Nonelectric guitar and electric bass

American Women 26.6%   Canadian Women 70.9%

---

*(N = 105)
**(N = 19)

trendsetting and hypercurrent. That MTV aired more than one video featuring several of these American artists further reinforces their elevated status. Successful celebrities receive heightened exposure, overshadowing other, less important performers.

But the distinctions do not end there. While Americans were presented as technologically wired, Canadians and other non-Americans were more often shown on both stations performing what Théberge calls "vintage" instruments (piano, violin), which serve to "give the player a form of direct sonic (and sometimes iconic) access to the past."[25] We already recognize the relationship between vintage instruments and the past in country and folk music genres where the harmonica and piano signify a connection to historical musicocultural traditions. That non-Americans play these instruments in the current sample, then, strengthens their connection to cultural lineage and memory, which cross-culturally and historically has been deemed one of women's important social tasks.[26]

I would argue that, when viewed in relation to the male-identified social construction of technology outlined previously, these representations are important because they perpetuate a previously established gendered metaphor of nationhood between Canada and the United States—a "feminized" Canada in relation to its "masculinized" American counterpart. This comparison is far from new. As Beverley Diamond has pointed out, this metaphor has a long history and extends across a range of public discourses, from nineteenth-century popular cartoon images of a feminized Miss Canada interacting with Uncle Sam, to common anthropormorphizations today such as the passive beaver and assertive eagle.[27] Indeed, this gendered contrast is deeply rooted within Canadian cultural expressions. Canadian literary theorist Northrop Frye has suggested that the image of Canada and its wilderness has functioned in distinguishing the country from its neighbor to the south. This image he describes is of two sexualized lands, whereby, as Eva Mackey suggests,

Frye . . . constructs Canada as a devouring, dangerous and alien female. . . . Part of this femaleness is that she is everywhere, unconquerable, and somehow not definite or definable. The USA, of the other hand, is more "male," more definite and phallic.[28]

From "high art" to popular culture, the metaphor of Canada as gendered female relative to the United States is pervasive. It could be suggested that the findings from the current sample corroborate this longstanding metaphor. Here, Canadian women projected a timbre and dynamic range that was "softer" than their American counterparts. This softness was accomplished through the use of acoustic instruments and representations of Canadians as performers of more "traditional" instruments. Of course, that the two stations tended to air different musical genres is in part responsible for these discrepancies: female instrumentalists on MTV (especially American instrumentalists) tended to perform alternative most often while the non-Canadians were associated with the pop genre. MTV viewers were exposed that week to timbrally edgier American women compared to the foreigners, giving them a more "definite" and self-assured identity.

I do not suggest that "Americanness" is always associated with these electrified genres and instruments. The musical signifier for the United States is slippery, and the country can be imagined just as readily through acoustic jazz timbres as it can through country music. How the United States "sounds" through a certain genre changes depending upon the social needs in particular historical moments. For instance: Aaron Fox argues that after September 11, 2001, country music came to stand in for "working-class" and "white" identity (which in turn became a replacement for "American" identity).[29] In other words, music as a signifier shifted according to new social needs: it became important after 9/11 for music to unify a wide range of listeners and invite people to think of "America" warmly and nostalgically. Country music was the perfect vehicle for this project. Similarly, Canada historically has been recognized at different moments for its singer-songwriter tradition (Gordon Lightfoot, Joni Mitchell, Murray McLaughlin), rock (Our Lady Peace, Tragically Hip, Bryan Adams) and female solo singers (Shania Twain, Celine Dion, k. d. lang, Sarah McLaughlin, Avril Lavigne, Alanis Morissette). Sometimes what is considered to represent a "Canadian sound" differs between cultural insiders and outsiders. Rock, for instance, has long been privileged within Canadian music history narratives, although it is often not the genre that signifies "Canadian popular music" abroad. At a benefit concert held in Toronto following September 11, 2001, for instance, headliners The Tragically Hip were introduced as "Canada's band," and celebrated that night as such. The Hip, however, has had far less international success and is less recognized internationally than many of the county's female solo singers. What broadly signifies the "Canadian genre" then can differ between different historical moments and differ between domestic and international audiences at the same time.[30]

It is crucial, then, to be context-specific when asking questions about musical signification, and during the week sampled in 1995, American female instrumentalists were defined not by their acoustic abilities, but by their electrification. That this definition placed the non-Americans in contrast opens the possibility that viewers—even unconsciously—could have extended this metaphor and interpreted American women to be socially more assertive than their foreign counterparts.

Performance Contexts/Celebrity Constructions

People from everywhere gather around
Checkin' out the sound that Eazy is throwin' down
—Eazy E, "We Want Eazy"

While the data on which and how often women instrumentalists are shown on the stations are useful when exploring women's representations in music video repertoires vis-à-vis gendering and celebrity construction, performance contexts may be argued to carry equal symbolic import. As Andrew Goodwin notes, the function of the performance footage for hard rock/heavy metal acts has been to establish

an "authentic" (i.e. documentary rather than fictional) set of images and to display musical competence. Thus "on the road" pseudodocumentaries and the use of close-ups to emphasize musical virtuosity became the main staples of the promotional clips.[31]

Not only do performance clips affect our perceptions of entire musical genres, they also often are intertwined with our reception of individual artists and their celebrity status. Viewers could perceive differences, for example, between two artists from the same genre, one of whom is frequently seen "live" in concert while the other is never shown performing in front of anyone. If a celebrity is an individual who is "known to be known," then the former artist might be perceived as a celebrity while the latter falls short of that status.

As noted above, live concert performance videos traditionally have been a mainstay for hard rock/heavy metal artists, a reflection of their desire for

Table 3.7

MTV: Percentage of Live Musical Performances Within Each Genre

Hard Rock/Metal	48.1%	(N = 51)
Urban	31.0%	(N = 144)
Industrial	20.0%	(N = 16)
Alternative	16.7%	(N = 263)
Reggae	16.7%	(N = 6)
Pop/Rock	10.0%	(N = 177)
Rock	6.1%	(N = 169)
Rap	1.7%	(N = 176)

musical "authenticity." Accordingly, I anticipated when I began my analysis of the data that the hard rock/metal genres—and, by extension, primarily male performers—would feature the most live concert performances. Indeed, on MTV, the hard rock/metal genre incorporated proportionally the most live musical performances. Table 3.7 indicates the percentage of videos featuring live concert performances within each genre.

Almost half (48.1 percent) of hard rock/metal videos shown on MTV featured live musical performances, followed by urban, industrial and alternative videos. These data seem to suggest that a viewer might perceive live musical performances as dominated by, although not exclusive to, heavy rock/metal artists. Yet, when the number of live musical performances per genre are considered in relation to the video repertoire overall, a different picture emerges. Hard rock/metal videos were not the largest contributors to live musical performances on MTV. Instead, urban and alternative videos were the most plentiful, as outlined in table 3.8.

The genres that featured the most live musical performances on MTV overall were urban and alternative with hard rock/metal falling in behind. If, as P. David Marshall has argued, the concert is the ritualization of the claim to authenticity and a celebration of community,[32] then it is important to consider *why* urban and alternative artists, like metal performers before them, dominated the video concert stage in videos from the sample. It is not likely that urban and alternative artists were striving to parallel the performer-audience relationships established by their metal peers: the urban video repertoire largely featured female artists exclusively or mixed-gender groups,[33] thus displacing the male-identification of the metal concert performance. Why urban and alternative videos aired on MTV were investing so heavily in the live concert image, admittedly, cannot be gained from the information provided thus far because it does not illuminate important particulars of the live performance context (including, for just two

Table 3.8

MTV: Number of Videos Featuring Live Musical Performances, by Genre

Video genre	Number of live performances
Urban	44
Alternative	44
Hard Rock/Metal	25
Pop/Rock	15
Rock	12
Industrial	2
Rap	3
Reggae	1

parameters, the size of the venue and the distance between artists and audience members). Any analysis of the type of community and hierarchical structures created within a musical performance venue hinges upon such information.

Because the musical performance settings for both alternative and urban videos varied considerably both within and across these genres, collapsing their components into three categories of "large," "medium," and "small" venues is highly reductive and does not take into account all of the video's nuances that may alter our perception of the artist's credibility. TLC's "Diggin' On You," for instance, is a live, large-venue performance video.[34] The sound, however, is a high-quality studio recording over which diegetic (or "actual") concert sounds are placed (at the opening of the video we hear the sounds of explosives as each performer "appears" on stage and, at the end of the video, applause is aligned with shots of the audience). Some viewers might not question this incongruity and simply enjoy the work; others might find that this discrepancy makes the video seem inauthentic. All videos are subject to criticism and skepticism to greater or lesser degrees because they incorporate prerecorded sounds. Some videos, however, might seem more credible because they are shot in smaller performance venues where the sound is more believable. Or, directors might include images of the musicians playing their own instruments, again, adding to the musicians' authenticity. Focusing the analysis to account only for venue sizes and excluding these other sonic/visual parameters limits the scope of what can be said about the artists' believability.

Nonetheless, dividing the repertoires into these three categories uncovers larger trends related to music genres that were evident in late 1995. For analytical consistency, a large-venue live musical performance is defined here as one that features the artist in an arena or stadium in front of many thousands of people.[35] A medium venue features an artist in a concert hall of several thousand people. A small venue is considerably more intimate; the artist is physically closer to the audience, and the audience numbers in the tens or hundreds rather than the thousands.

When divided into large, medium, and small-venue formats, a significant pattern emerges within the alternative category. A total of forty-four alternative videos featured live musical performances; thirty-eight (86.4 percent) of these were set within small venues. A few examples illustrate this more intimate style: the *MTV Unplugged* concert version of Nirvana's "All Apologies" is recorded in front of a visibly small audience; Weezer's "Buddy Holly" is set within the *Happy Days* setting, again in front of a small audience.[36] Only three alternative videos featured live, large-venue performance contexts: Pearl Jam's "Alive," Nine Inch Nails' "Hurt," and Sonic Youth's "The Diamond Sea." The pervasiveness of the small venue reflects the origins (and ongoing desired image) of the alternative scene as one that is shy of commercial success. It also serves to mask the massive scale on which alternative music is performed, disseminated, and consumed by the alternative viewer who may be critical of commercial "sellout."

The number of urban live performances equaled that of the alternative category (44). The significant difference, however, is the high number of large-venue performance urban videos (65.9 percent), with small venues totaling 34.1 percent of the genre. This figure arose, in part, from the frequency with which TLC's "Diggin' On You," a gigantic concert video, was aired that week alongside Salt-N-Pepa's "Push It." The few small-venue videos were Deborah Cox's "Sentimental," Xscape's "Who Can I Run To," and TLC's "Creep."

If we shift the perspective and organize these urban videos according to the artists' gender and nationality, more details emerge. On MTV, all live urban videos featured female artists (no male urban performers were featured in a live performance setting); 91.1 percent of these performers were American women and 8.9 percent were non-American performers. This 8.9 percent was in fact only one (repeated) video, "Sentimental," featuring Canadian singer Deborah Cox. Set in a lounge environment, Cox sings to the patrons who listen comfortably while seated around round tables. The only video featuring a non-American urban-genre woman, then, featured her within a small and intimate setting. Conversely, the only videos to feature the artists within a large-venue live urban musical performance were American.

What is significant about this modest collection of five large- and small-venue musical performance urban videos is that they all featured black female performers (not one white female artist performed within a live setting within any genre). These five videos then, constituting forty-four video air-ings, collectively signify a shift in power. P. David Marshall, departing from the traditional correlation between live musical performances and authen-ticity, has outlined the various types of power inherent in a live setting that might be informative for understanding the present repertoire. I outline below three points that are important for the present analysis.

First, Marshall suggests that the live musical performance aligns the "committed" performer with the power of the crowd:

or, more accurately, provides for the public sphere a representation of the embodi-ment of the crowd and the crowd's power in contemporary culture. . . . [This] makes the rock star an alluring representative of cultural power.[37]

Second, beyond the artist's role in representing the crowd, Marshall notes that the appearance of a large crowd gives the impression that the artist represents *something*, whether that is simply the group itself, and/or an ideology with political or social import.[38] Such was the case for many art-ists who initiated moral panic (Elvis, the Rolling Stones, the Sex Pistols, and more recently, Marilyn Manson).[39] Marshall, again:

The celebrity, then, represents the potential for societal transformation or even the catalyst for its breakdown . . . the popular music celebrity . . . is often the public rep-resentation of change. The large crowds . . . serve to substantiate the organization of power behind these representatives of change.[40]

Third and finally, the crowd itself can also symbolically represent the artists' access to economic capital vis-à-vis the concert, music, and other miscellaneous sales.[41] This success, in turn, can be read as an avenue to additional artistic freedom, and the ability of the artist to make more of his creative choices, which could then be used for particular ends. (These opportunities have been evidenced over the past several years by artists like Madonna starting the Maverick label and having more control over her own image and musical output, or Geri Halliwell taking managerial control over, and subsequently leaving, the Spice Girls for other career endeavors. Both cases speak to the artistic allowances permitted to eco-nomically successful performers.) The larger the audience within the pop/urban music video, the more financially successful the artist may be per-ceived to be by the viewing audience. That black female artists were foregrounded within the live, primarily large-venue setting, then, sig-naled financial success and possible social significance. In the particular case of TLC, their importance was heightened in "Diggin' on You" by their arrival in a helicopter, while their confidence/professionalism is communicated implicitly. They needed only to arrive within hours or even minutes of their performance.

TLC's enormous success, of course, extends beyond their video representations. With their second album, *Crazysexycool*, TLC outsold The Supremes, earning the title of world's all-time best-selling female group to that date. Yet, a review of popular writing on the group suggests that they were largely excluded from the discourse surrounding the most pervasive phase of youth culture during the second half of the decade: "girl power." The honor of globalizing "girl power" usually falls upon the Spice Girls, whose 1996 debut unit *Spice* was close on the heels of TLC's success. What is striking about recent writings on the Spice Girls and their manifestation of "girl power" is the link between that group and their alternative predecessors; that is, their lineage within a predominantly white demographic. Of course, these writings are entirely accurate. Gayle Wald rightly points out that the Spice Girls' clearly appropriated the defiant English riot grrls' style,[42] and Catherine Driscoll traces their style to the aesthetics of Hole, Bikini Kill, and other alternative groups.[43] But alternative grrls' contribution to the Spice aesthetic—musical and otherwise—was limited in several significant ways. First, their edgy alternative timbres and gutsy lyrics were not ideal for marketing to the preteen market, and the Spice Girls were targeted to this group (in fact, they are considered to be the first band to allow 4-, 5-, and 6-year-old girls to own their own music).[44] Second, riot grrls have never had significant exposure vis-à-vis extramusical merchandise, whereas the Spice Girls profited enormously from their line of stickers, posters, magazines, and clothing that targeted the 4-year-old through teenage demographic. Here is where black urban and rap artists played a significant role in preparing the North American audience, with their smooth, self-assured, heavily marketed image that enjoyed heavy rotation on MTV's playlists prior to the Spice Girls' emergence.

TLC's highly sexualized images and lyric content were more explicit than those of the Spice Girls and therefore might have limited their potential for forwarding "girl power"—especially to very young female audiences. Take but a few examples: "Diggin' on You," a "live" performance video, contains unambiguous sexual gestures. In the bridge prior to the last fade-out of choruses, Chilli (Rozonda Thomas) takes the lead while T-Boz (Tionne Watkins) and Left Eye (Lisa Lopes) sing backup to the text: "What was it in a line / That made me fall for you / Do You know / Why I'm diggin' diggin' diggin' diggin' on you." During the last line—"diggin'"— the three vocalists lean back; two move their microphones suggestively between their legs, evoking heterosexual intercourse.

"Red Light Special," which was aired on MTV in late 1995, features another sexually charged text.[45] "Red Light" presents lead singer T-Boz with the group in several musical performance and narrative settings. In the first setting, T-Boz sings in a color-saturated room while a man undresses and seduces her; a second context features the group playing a game of strip poker with a group of men (shot in color and black and white). The lyrics, meanwhile, are highly suggestive: "I'll let you touch it if you'd / Like to go down / I'll let you go further / If you take the southern route." The text and images reinforce the title's clear reference to sexual availability. At the close of the video, a disagreement transpires between the participants in the strip poker game; Left Eye, the group member with the reputation for revenge, overturns the card table.

It was images like the overturning card table that prepared us for the Spice Girls and their upcoming "rebellious" antics. The Spice Girls, the group with whom "girl power" came to be musically associated in the 1990s, defined the term as playfully demanding ("I'll tell you what I want, what I really, really want"), emphasizing the importance of strong female relationships. Comedian Chris Rock may have challenged the value of the Spice Girls on the 1997 MTV Awards (indeed, this girl group received considerable criticism, a good deal of which was unwarranted), but these five women were what the music industries were seeking: they were mostly white, and less sexually provocative (and therefore less socially dangerous) than TLC, thus potentially reaching a larger audience demographic. The cultural media advanced their brand of "third-wave feminism" as a fresh and spunky contribution to the pop music genre.

The appearance of black women in live settings, of course, did more than set the stage for a new "feminist" aesthetic: it also created the impression of black female economic capital. Having lived in the shadows of white and black male artists on MTV, the emergence of powerful black female groups—not only through their sexual images but as "successful" live performing artists—was indicative, ideologically speaking, of an important social shift. Of course, within the context of MTV, it is not unreasonable to suggest that these adoring crowds were visible in order to construct the *perception* of social change. These girl groups were intentionally positioned at the forefront to inject an always-needed freshness into the music industry.

But these black girl groups served a second agenda. They were also part of MTV's larger shift from hard-core rap to less oppositional forms of musics featuring black artists in the mid-1990s. This trajectory begins with the 1988 introduction of *Yo! MTV Raps. Yo!* premiered on Saturdays with Fab 5 Freddy as host. Several months later it expanded to the weekday edition, featuring Ed Lover and rap producer/writer/performer Doctor Dre. *Yo!* quickly became one of MTV's highest-rated shows. According to Ted Demme, who then worked at MTV: "The show was getting great ratings and really good press. . . . MTV [was] happy when there was a certain type of rap . . . [like] D.J. Jazzy Jeff and the Fresh Prince . . . but when [the group] N.W.A. came up, and rap started to get gangsta . . . MTV's standards went berserk."[46] What Demme suggests here is that once gangsta rap began to receive airplay, MTV, fearing a backlash, pulled back on this programming. In 1992, Demme left the show. After his departure, the program timeslot was shifted around until it finally was moved to the midnight to 2 A.M. Saturday morning time slot in January 1993. In 1995, hosts Freddy, Lover, and Dre were relieved of hosting duties. *Yo! MTV Raps* then became even less identifiable, featuring different weekly hosts inconsistently aired within the designated Saturday morning slot. Inconsistent VJ appearances coupled with irregular scheduling jeopardized viewer-program identification, resulting, predictably, in low viewer ratings. As Carter Harris has noted, by the mid-1990s, MTV was substituting cutting-edge (primarily male) rap music of the early 1990s with "softer" black music (with a healthy injection of female artists like TLC and Brandy) on programs like *MTV Jams* and within the general video flow.[47] This repertoire of highly visible black female urban artists facilitated an easier removal of higher-risk rap artists, allowing MTV to be seen to program black artists (although these artists were carefully chosen so as not to disrupt the social status quo).

On MuchMusic, meanwhile, both similar and different live musical performance patterns were evidenced, patterns that speak particularly to the Canadian context. First, male artists were featured within a live musical performance setting in ninety-five videos. The three largest groups were Americans, with thirty-two videos; British groups, with nineteen videos; and Canadians, with thirteen videos. What is striking about this list is that the American repertoire included large live musical performance venues (for example, Guns N' Roses, "Paradise City," or Hootie and the Blowfish, "Time"), as did the Australian and British repertoires (AC/DC, "Hard as a Rock," and Def Leppard, "I Wanna Touch You," respectively). All of the live musical performance videos including Canadian males, however, featured small venues, with two exceptions: Neil Young's "All Along the Watchtower," which is set in a medium-size venue (it does not qualify as a "stadium performance"), and Bonnie Raitt and Bryan Adams's "Rock Steady" which was similarly set in a medium-size concert hall.

These findings raise two points. First, no Canadian male "qualifies" for the status required for a stadium performance, although two well-known rock musicians, Young and Adams, are given higher celebrity status than their Canadian male peers vis-à-vis venue size. The second point—the data pertaining to women's live musical performance—is even more striking. Not one video featuring a Canadian female performer presented her in front of a live concert audience; instead, all live videos that foregrounded women featured either American or European performers. One video featuring a Canadian artist did come close: Quebecois artist Julie Masse's video "Prends bien garde" was filmed in a large-stage concert setting, but without a single camera shot of an audience. The audience's presence is implicit, however, when Masse waves to them before leaving the stage. Masse's "invisible audience," which bears the closest resemblance to a live Canadian crowd, conveys disparaging information regarding Canadian women's celebrity construction, social importance, and commercial success. Its absence also speaks to the weak cultural capital held by Canadian audiences in this video and beyond.[48]

According to Denise Donlon, director of programming at MuchMusic in 1995, live concert videos are not so viable for Canadian performers because of the high production costs and because Canada has too small an economic base to amortize the initial investment. Moreover, Donlon feels that live musical performance videos generally have a shorter shelf live, making them less attractive for producers. "It just may be simple economics," explains Donlon.[49] Nonetheless, it is interesting that *no* Canadian artists appeared live within large venues (absent from this sample were internationally known performers like k. d. lang, Celine Dion, or Roch Voisine). The lack of Canadian concert videos does reflect an economic reality, but I would argue that this absence in turn perpetuates a well-known domestic narrative: Canadians have a complicated—and often frustrated—relationship with home-grown celebrity.

For a number of possible reasons—economic status, cultural notions of celebrity, musical genre—Bryan Adams and Neil Young were the only two Canadians to perform on MuchMusic in a medium-sized live concert setting. This underrepresentation of Canadians as performing icons might not be surprising to the Canadian viewer. The notion of the Canadian celebrity has long been viewed as an oxymoron. From the Canadian Broadcasting Corporation's unwillingness to develop a Canadian television star system to the absence of an internationally recognized (resident) Canadian film star, the notion of the Canadian celebrity is perpetually frustrated. This is not to say Canadian-born personalities do not succeed once they move abroad (Mike Myers, Jim Carrey, Shania Twain, Alanis Morissette), but they are often perceived domestically as exactly that: Canadian-*born* performers. Achieving celebrity status often means becoming enveloped within the American star system, moving abroad (usually to the United States), and losing the distinction as an "authentic" Canadian; that is, one who stays at home. Greg Potter calls this the "Canadian pop-rock paradox." The quest for international celebrity usually results in the artists' loss of Canadian identity.[50] If achieving and maintaining "Canadianness" means a refusal of the celebrity system predominant within the United States, and music video is one key to manufacturing and disrupting the star system, then it may not be insignificant that live video performances featuring Canadian and American artists differed so drastically on the two stations.

In this chapter I have explored an important cultural narrative: the "masculinized" American nation-state relative to its "feminized" neighbor to the north. I have established how this narrative was corroborated in the stations' video repertoires vis-à-vis women, instrumentation, and live performances. The electric guitar was the most commonly played instrument by women on MTV and these musicians largely were Americans; on MuchMusic, women played electric bass most often and, in addition to other electric instruments, they also were represented playing a wider range of acoustic ("vintage") instruments—more so than their American counterparts. Here, then, are clear connections on both stations among American identity, technology, currency, volume, instrumentation, and social space, which, when combined, tie in to preexisting cultural myths of what it means to be an American (versus a more "passive" Canadian). Further, American artists occasionally appeared in more than just one video on MTV, which contributed to a stronger sense of celebrity. That Americans—both men and women—were shown performing in front of a live audience and within larger venues also contributes to a sense of celebrity and the cultural power that holds. When Canadians did perform in front of audiences the venues were small; in the case of the one video by Julie Masse, the audience was not even noteworthy enough to be shown on camera.

Although MTV and MuchMusic aired different repertoires that week, their videos that featured women instrumentalists and women performing in "live" venues conveyed a remarkably similar message. These videos corroborated a popular—and sometimes dangerous—gendered discourse that differentiates our national ideologies, one that is perpetuated with enthusiasm on either side of the forty-ninth parallel. It is important to acknowledge the extent to which this powerful narrative constructs both countries' sense of national identity and, in turn, actually shapes and justifies our social and political policies both at home and abroad. It is told to us on a daily basis through the popular media and perpetuated on MTV and MuchMusic, even unknowingly, in something as seemingly benign as a week of music videos.

CHAPTER FOUR

Multiculturalism, Diversity, and Containment

*For MTV, the existence of a culture of the mass is deeply problematic, since it
questions the fundamental mode of its distribution and consumption. The domestic, rather than the mass, is the given on which MTV predicates its signification as well as its business practices. Its racism is not a simple prejudice but a
product of a struggle over the mode of circulation of meanings in the suburban,
atomised and monopoly-dominated model of cultural formation.*
— Sean Cubitt, *Timeshift*

It's the format.
—MTV

"Pluralistic" is not an adjective that applies easily to the early years of
MTV. Accusations of exclusionary practices date back to 1983 when MTV
was criticized explicitly for excluding black artists. As Carter Harris
argues, while MTV claimed to be playing "anything that could be called
rock 'n' roll" in its early years, few black artists actually were featured.[1]
Richard Gold similarly criticized MTV's imbalance when he stated in
1982 that "r&b artists in general continue to remain on the periphery of
the music video revolution."[2] Rolling Stone's 1983 statistics corroborated
both authors' observations. During MTV's first eighteen months, fewer
than two dozen videos—of the 750 aired—featured black artists.[3] As a de-
fense against these accusations MTV argued that black artists' music did
not suit the desired format, meaning that white audiences would not
enjoy this music. As Bob Pittman, founder of MTV stated, "[W]e turned
down Rick James because the consumer didn't define him as rock."[4] Les
Garland, an MTV executive during the early 1980s, argued alongside Pittman for the merits of a narrower repertoire, "You cannot be all things to
all people. You cannot play jazz and country music and funk. You lose
your focus."[5]

As the now famous sequence of events goes, pressure continued to mount on the station to air more black artists. Following David Bowie's 1983 interview with VJ Mark Goodman—during which the marginalization of black artists on MTV and the success of Michael Jackson's *Thriller* was raised (*Thriller* was the bestselling album of all time with seven Top 10 U.S. singles)[6]—the "racial barrier" was chipped away to the extent that black artists were aired more frequently. Nonetheless, by 1986, a few years after Jackson's breakthrough, underrepresentation was still a point of contention and remained under scrutiny. Brown and Campbell's (1986) content analysis of MTV, for instance, revealed that nonwhite featured singers or bandleaders of either gender only accounted for 5 percent of all videos aired.[7] They concluded that white men were almost always the focal point while black artists—and all women—were rarely important enough to be foregrounded at all.[8]

During the late 1980s and early 1990s, MTV significantly increased the number of black artists aired within the video flow, thanks in part to public response to a number of successful MTV programs showcasing black artists, most notably the highly popular *Yo! MTV Raps*.[9] Other key developments that strengthened the position of black artists during the 1980s included the emergence of crossover music—which combines historically black (rap) and white (rock) genres—and the success of rap itself, reflected by the success of *Yo! MTV Raps*. Indeed, in 1993 video scholar Andrew Goodwin suggested that because of such important strides "the question of racism [on MTV] has been resolved."[10]

While these changes at MTV are impressive on paper, we have reason to be skeptical, particularly given the station's early track record. What the data do not provide, for instance, is insight into how the station may have increased programming for black artists while simultaneously or subsequently containing their artistic growth. For instance, while *Yo!* was a boost for black artists, it is not coincidental that its 1988 debut followed the crossover triumph of white artists into black-dominated rap. Run-D.M.C. and Aerosmith's 1986 hit "Walk this Way" reached number four on the pop charts, providing Aerosmith, one of the most successful rock bands of the 1970s, with a musical comeback through a brief interlude into rap. In late 1986 The Beastie Boys, a hardcore New York punk band, crossed into hard rock and rap and released *Licensed to Ill*, which became the first rap album to reach number one. While these artists should be credited with bringing rap to the white masses, their contributions may simultaneously have been used by MTV to render this black genre "safer" or "more familiar" for white youth, echoing Elvis's R&B contribution some thirty years earlier. While *Yo! MTV Raps* was indeed an inclusive, validating gesture towards black artists and rap, we can also see it as a means for corporate MTV to shape a young underground musical tradition, choosing "appropriate" rap styles and artists for their viewers. On the point of racial inclusivity, Homi Bhabha offers an important observation: while "multicultural" societies encourage diversity, this gesture frequently is accompanied by modes of containment and control. Under these circumstances, "the universalism that paradoxically permits diversity masks ethnocentric norms, values and interests."[11] In other words, racism does not disappear but simply takes more cleverly disguised forms. In question here is what forms racism takes on MTV and how the inclusion of black performers has simultaneously been counteracted with containment practices.

While MTV has endured considerable criticism for its relationship with black artists, MuchMusic has received very little critical attention on issues of race and marginalization. Because less overall attention has been paid to MuchMusic in popular magazines, newspapers, and scholarly journals since its inception in 1984, this observation is not entirely surprising. Nonetheless, as the literature on Canadian multiculturalism and cultural plurality expands, MuchMusic continues to remain outside of the pertinent debates. Does this suggest that MuchMusic, regulated at the governmental level by a Canadian multicultural social policy, has found a solution to the problems with which MTV has struggled all these years? Is it possible that the Canadian station has celebrated multicultural expression rather than try to suppress it? Or, because it is a Canadian product, have media analysts dismissed it as less important, and therefore less dangerous than MTV, allowing it to escape critical attention unscathed?

MTV

While MTV has unquestionably increased the number of black performers over the past several decades, journalists have argued that the artists and types of videos shown on the station gradually have changed. As mentioned in the previous chapter, Carter Harris has argued that a number of MTV shows featuring oppositional black performers have been rendered less accessible on the station. This, he suggests, is the history of *Yo! MTV Raps*. In 1995, reggae artists experienced similar processes of marginalization. The week of my sample, MTV aired four reggae videos; all but one was shown on the program *Reggae Sound System*. Shot in Jamaica, *Sound System* was a thirteen-part series supposedly aimed at expanding the network's black diasporic programming by showcasing different styles of dancehall, dub, and reggae. The show faced difficulties from the outset and experienced airing delays. Finally, it was shown in the fall of 1995, between

1:30 and 2 A.M. on Tuesday mornings, a time slot clearly unfavorable for attracting a large viewing audience. As producer Jac Benson stated, "I don't see how my show is supposed to survive and be successful at this hour . . . this show represents a year and a half of work, and this is what it gets?"[12]

I would have to agree with Harris when he suggests that MTV increasingly has demonstrated a preference for "softer" (that is, safer) music showcasing black artists such as Boyz II Men, squeezing out N.W.A. and *Yo! MTV Raps*.[13] Whereas MTV was known in the late 1980s for its daring programming featuring controversial, oppositional artists, it became more likely to air "palatable" soft urban performers. If, then, MTV has simultaneously increased the number of black artists while pulling videos that provide social critique and/or express cultural diversity, it is difficult to agree with Goodwin that the "racism question" has been answered in a meaningful way.

MuchMusic

MuchMusic had to face much more stringent policies on cultural inclusion when it was launched than did MTV, and it continues to do so today. These policies were established by the CRTC, who was responsible, among other things, for licensing stations and enforcing regulations such as the Canadian content quota and multicultural representation. According to the CRTC policy on cultural diversity, for instance, MuchMusic must "reflect . . . the multicultural and multiracial nature of Canadian society."[14] The CRTC has been pleased with MuchMusic's efforts. In 2000, they commended the station "for its efforts to reflect and portray fairly the rich ethnic diversity of Canadians."[15] I agree with the CRTC that MuchMusic should be commended for airing videos far beyond the mainstream repertoire. MuchMusic regularly featured a world music show entitled *Cliptrip,* as well as *MuchEast* and *MuchWest,* programs showcasing lesser known music and musicians from Canada's outlying regions. The economic challenges in programming music with less economic return are significant. As Avi Lewis, a former MuchMusic host, stated, "to create spaces for different genres of music and unusual music that won't find its way into the mainstream because it'll never be that commercially successful is always an effort. It's always . . . a process of advocacy."[16] Indeed, MuchMusic foregrounds cultural and racial diversity significantly more than does MTV, and this programming frequently intersects with explicit forms of social criticism.

While MTV excluded non-American rap artists the week of my sample and thus linked rap exclusively with the United States, MuchMusic featured a more pluralistic repertoire within which artists critiqued sociopolitical constructs. Videos featuring Canadian rappers the Dream Warriors serve as an example. As Rinaldo Walcott has pointed out, the music of the Warriors illustrates how black migratory histories, policies, and experiences are constantly renegotiated, challenging socially defined constructs of nation, home, and family.[17] This challenge includes the Warriors' practice of naming places in the Caribbean and Canada in their songs and celebrating black diasporic connections, thus creating a space of the "in-between."[18] In their song "My Definition of a Boombastic Jazz Style,"[19] for example, they sample the "Definition" theme song, familiar to many Canadians as the music from the 1970s television game show of the same name. They simultaneously quote from Quincy Jones. The song therefore is about being both a Canadian and part of the rich transnational black diaspora. The "Definition" the Warriors seek to clarify, of course, is not only musical: "I walk with a gold cane, a gold brain, and no gold chain. . . . Your definition of me is definitely wrong / Why must I try to lie and find an alibi / When all you ask is just for me to be me." Combining a theme historically linked with Canadian popular culture while questioning their own "definition," the Warriors meaningfully problematize identity and belonging.

Similarly, the Warriors' song "Day In Day Out" from the 1995 sample is situated clearly within the Canadian landscape by the deliberate inclusion of one of the most familiar icons—the CN Tower—alongside images of Toronto city streets. I do not suggest that these artists identify with this icon and buy into the notion of being "at home" within the Canadian nation-state. By the end of the song, the rappers turn their attention lyrically beyond Canadian imagery, paying homage to those who started hip-hop "when hip hop was hip hop," by naming groups like Public Enemy and other performers from England, Canada, and the United States. Visually, the Warriors are positioned within Canada but they extend beyond the country's boundaries lyrically by tracing their musical lineage vis-à-vis non-Canadian performers of the black diaspora. Here the Warriors express the frustration of many Canadian rappers who feel doubly displaced, perceived as outsiders and not full "owners" of Canadian identity but also not "owners" of rap: a prevalent perception within the United States is that rap was and continues to be an essentially American genre.[20] Accordingly, Canadian rappers such as the Dream Warriors articulate their concerns and construct their identities differently, and sometimes in more complex ways, than their American peers.

MuchMusic, then, could be perceived as a mouthpiece for rap discourses that extend beyond American-identified experiences to the problematics of the black diaspora within Canada. Indeed, black national identifications are not limited to these two countries on MuchMusic. A number of videos aired within the sample also emphasized notions of Afrocentricity (the foregrounding of Africa and the experiences of people of the African diaspora) through sonic and/or visual imagery. For instance, Afrika Bambaataa's "Sho Nuff Funky," a live musical performance video featuring Bambaataa and Family, invokes Africa through explicit visual references, including silhouettes of Africa hanging in the concert hall and on the neck-lace of one of the singers. Other videos were linked with Africa through a combination of texts. In James Brown's and Afrika Bambaataa's funk video "Unity," Afrocentricity lines the work both musically and lyrically.[21] First, Afrocentricity is manifest musically. Funk, as Rob Bowman argues, was in itself a musical manifestation of the re-Africanization movement of black culture within the United States during the late 1960s. It was James Brown who, beginning with "Cold Sweat" (1967), de-emphasized features such as melody and harmony (commonly associated with Euro-American music-making) and foregrounded syncopated and interlocking grooved rhythms (associated with sub-Saharan Africa).[22] Although Brown has stated that he sees no connection between African music and his own,[23] for many black Americans, funk signified not only a pro-black musical articulation, but an important connection with Africa itself. These musical/cultural connec-tions with funk similarly underlie "Unity."

Also entwined in Brown's musical performance of "Cold Sweat" was the notion of community, evidenced in his process of naming band members and his intense commitment to the audience.[24] Brown did not demand top billing during the musical performance but situated himself parallel to the other musicians present.[25] A parallel argument could be made for Brown and Bambaataa in "Unity." The words "peace," "unity," "love," and "hav-ing fun" appear on the screen to reinforce visually the lyric content. These words reappear periodically in a number of languages, communicating to the English-speaking viewer their desire for unity both locally and transna-tionally. The artists address the need for common positive goals within the international "community," an extension of the local community articu-lated and honored in "Cold Sweat."

The video aired on MuchMusic that makes the most explicit reference to Afrocentrism is Queen Latifah's "Ladies First."[26] This video has been ana-lyzed with attention to its strong feminist agenda. As Robin Roberts has pointed out, "Ladies First" is also a clear articulation of Latifah's Afrocen-tricity.[27] This interpretation should not be surprising. Latifah repeatedly has stated her commitment to raising awareness and paying homage to her African heritage: "To me Afrocentricity is a way of living. . . . It's about being into yourself and into your people and being proud of your ori-gins."[28] The video affirms the connections between African Americans and

Africa in a number of ways. First, it opens with images of women who have advanced political reform. Second, it includes a picture of a young Winnie Mandela among images of distinguished African American women. Finally, the video includes South African images that address apartheid and struggle.[29] The video also references Africa through Latifah's dress: a military uniform with red, black, and green that evoke the colors of the African National Congress.[30] As Roberts has pointed out, between Latifah's attire and her physical actions of destroying large cement fists placed on a map of South Africa, she identifies herself as a participant in the ongoing struggle against racism and imperialism.[31]

George Lipsitz and Timothy Brennan have taken up discussions on the political successes and limitations of Latifah's video. Writing first, Lipsitz argues that this work is unique and progressive because it establishes common diasporic global links between, among others, South African political resistors and American teenagers, and made a minority population of the United States part of a global struggle, a project that had eluded Latifah's rap predecessors.[32] Brennan has countered Lipsitz, arguing that there is no such thing as a common diasporic meaning, and that at the same time Latifah's video incorporates footage of revolts and protest in South African townships, it domesticates these images for its own purposes. While the video's images can be argued to be informative and therefore empowering for American youth, the struggle represented in the video is not comparable to the struggle itself, and there is a danger in suggesting that it is. South Africa therefore becomes part of a commodified American "image-for-use" text that expands awareness of the South African apartheid protest movement while simultaneously containing it.[33]

"Ladies First" clearly can be read in multifarious ways, and that is what makes it such a rich and important video. When combined with "Sho Nuff Funky" and "Unity," it creates a small yet important handful of videos that make connections between the performers and their African roots, visually, textually, and/or sonically. Because MuchMusic's entire video repertoire is historically broader than MTV's, early videos such as "Unity" (1984), "Sho Nuff Funky" (1988), and "Ladies First" (1990)—which make explicit, and sometimes controversial, references to Afrocentricity—held a solid and not atypical place within their video rotation. The first two videos were shown twice on MuchMusic during an after-school program entitled *Rap City,* which was then repeated during the late-night rotation from 1:30 to 2:00 A.M. Queen's Latifah's video, meanwhile, was shown on a general video flow segment on an early Monday afternoon and again the next morning, before school for most viewers. These airing times, then, were considerably more accessible than MTV's *Reggae Sound System,* thus potentially drawing a larger audience than if they were shown only at marginalized times. These videos are also significant because some of them, particularly those featuring Queen Latifah and the aforementioned Dream Warriors, critique political relations and their identities as persons of the African diaspora within North America. Their efforts create what Bhabha would call a "third space" (a hybrid space) that "displaces the histories that constitute it, and sets up new structures of authority, [and] new political initiatives."[34] None of the videos discussed here—or related videos that similarly create a "third space"—appeared on MTV during the sample.

MuchMusic's video repertoire and scheduling, meanwhile, also evidence particular modes of restriction and containment. Because MuchMusic's programming over the 1980s and 1990s has not been so scrutinized as MTV's, specific changes in programming trends are not so well documented. Accordingly, I have chosen instead to analyze MuchMusic's 1995 repertoire through one of the traditionally most contained video repertoires: highly choreographed (dance) videos. Indeed, from the mid-1980s into the 1990s, dance was largely the domain of marginalized subgroups in mainstream music videos—black artists and women, while the more dominant subgroups, particularly white men, almost always featured the musician/vocalist.

An analysis of the MTV Top 100 videos from 1985 to 1994 (the top ten from each year) evidenced that only rarely did white males dance. Most often they incorporated dance in their videos featuring other, more marginalized performers.[35] In Tears for Fears' video "Everybody Wants to Rule the World" (1985, no. 7), for instance, co-lead singer Roland Orzabal sings and plays guitar in a studio, while smiling at footage of two black male dancers. Here, dance is relegated to minorities while (voyeuristically) enjoyed by the white male artists. In R.E.M.'s "Stand" (1989, no. 7), white men dance (significantly not the band members) but the dance simultaneously is trivialized with humor. In fact, only two white male musicians performed their own dances within these hundred videos: George Harrison in "I've Got My Mind Set On You" (1988, no. 8) and Vanilla Ice in "Ice Ice Baby" (1990, no. 7). Harrison's video, like R.E.M.'s, is characterized by a comedic tone; objects within the room "come to life" and "lip sync" along with him. This aesthetic is unusual as the lyrics do not reflect this affect. Harrison's acrobatic dance (actually performed by a stand-in) reinforces the video's silliness. The viewing audience in 1988 clearly was not supposed to take seriously the first instance of a white male performing a dance segment within this repertoire.

Vanilla Ice's performance, unlike Harrison's, initially appears more genuine. Ice's interest in dance is linked to his strong desire to be adopted within the rap community. Ice previously had engaged in other ploys to gain acceptance. In 1991, it was disclosed that he had misrepresented himself in his record company's biography: his status as working class was forged in order to be more palatable to rap audiences.[36] That he dances in his video is not surprising. It is an obvious extension of his desire to place himself within the traditions of hip-hop culture and simultaneously work against the expectations of white male performers.

White male artists, then, did not embrace dance during this decade-long span, at least not within the most "successful" video repertoire, the MTV Top 100 list. If one of dance's functions at the end of the 1980s was as an access mode for black males and females, and white females, and these groups were, by the mid-1990s, more intrinsic to the mainstream video repertoire, who performed highly choreographed dance in late 1995? Was it more balanced among the demographics? Did these statistics differ between the MTV and MuchMusic repertoires?

For comparative purposes, the coding process used here separates three levels of movement, from the most simple to the most complex. The first level recognizes movement as a gesture: here, dance is for the personal pleasure of the musicians or audience, where no obvious choreography exists. The second, or organized-movement level, features dance as an accompanying text, a temporary focus of the video that is superseded in importance by another text (such as the music). Finally, the choreographed style features a more complex dance vocabulary wherein the motions are rehearsed and replicable, and function as a highly expressive tool.

Within the current sample, particular subgroups consistently perform these three movement levels. Table 4.1 outlines these levels according to white and black males and females, on both stations.

Table 4.1
MTV and MuchMusic: Choreographic Movement Levels by Gender and Race

	White males	White females	Black males	Black females
*MTV**				
Choreography	1.0%	8.4%	6.4%	34.8%
Organized movement	6.1%	13.7%	46.5%	38.4%
Gesture	92.9%	77.9%	47.1%	26.8%
*MuchMusic***				
Choreography	2.6%	19.4%	14.2%	63.3%
Organized movement	5.4%	5.6%	33.1%	10.1%
Gesture	92.0%	75.0%	52.7%	26.6%

*MTV: WM (N = 409), WF (N = 131), BM (N = 140), BF (N = 138).
**MuchMusic: WM (N = 786), WF (N = 178), BM (N = 165), BF (N = 79).

These data point to commonalities and differences between the two stations' repertoires. A brief glance across the tables indicates that gesture for all four groups did not vary considerably between the two stations. Discrepancies are clearer between the stations within the organized movement and choreographic categories. Of particular interest are the data on choreography: white males were predictably low in this category and consistently so between the two stations (1.0 percent on MTV and 2.6 percent on MuchMusic). White females varied significantly more (8.4 percent on MTV and 19.4 percent on MuchMusic). Black males also differed slightly: 6.4 percent of the videos featuring black males on MTV included choreographed dance as opposed to 14.2 percent on MuchMusic. The largest discrepancy between the two stations involved black women: 34.8 percent of the time black women appeared on MTV they featured choreographed dance; this figure was a staggering 63.3 percent on MuchMusic.

These data indicate that choreographed dance remained an activity dominated by marginalized subgroups—and especially black women—on both stations that week. That these dancers largely appeared as sexualized objects through dress and bodily gestures seems to corroborate what Patricia Hill Collins observed previously on a central function of black women within music video texts:

In the early 1990s, the *celebration* of Black women's bodies . . . that had long appeared in earlier Black cultural production . . . became increasingly replaced by the *objectification* of Black women's bodies as part of a commodified Black culture. . . . The women in these videos typically share two attributes—they are rarely acknowledged as individuals and they are scantily clad. One Black female body can easily replace another and all are reduced to their bodies [emphasis original].[37]

Because these interchangeable bodies saturated the mass media in 1995—as they do today in even more extreme representations—they were and continue to be rendered almost invisible. Yet, black women's narrow hypersexualization continues to be perpetuated through an emphasis on large breasts, permissive clothing, the "booty" and sexually explicit lyrics—all largely produced for the young male viewer's gaze.[38]

Here we acknowledge the representational pitfalls when dance becomes the domain of a particular marginalized subgroup. But the activity in itself, of course, is not always disempowering. In *Gender Politics and MTV: Voicing the Difference* (1990), Lisa Lewis argues that dance can function positively in female-address videos as "access signs" or "discovery signs." She defines access signs as those "in which the privileged experiences of boys and men are visually appropriated . . . [s]ymbolically, they execute takeovers of male space . . . and make demands for parity with male-adolescent privilege."[39] Pat Benetar's "Love is a Battlefield" is such an example.[40] The video depicts a homeless female teenager on the street; the narrative moves to the inside of a bar (a male space) where a woman screams in fear. A group of women break out with aggressive gestures to protect the teenager while the lyrics announce "We are strong / no one can tell us we're wrong." According to Lewis, within this video dance is a powerful symbol of female militancy.[41]

Lewis's second category consists of "discovery signs" that "refer to and celebrate distinctly female modes of cultural expression and experience." As she states, "These signs attempt to compensate for the devaluation and triv-ialization of female-cultural experience by presenting images of activities that are shared by girls alone."[42] Lewis argues for dance in Cyndi Lauper's "Girls Just Wanna Have Fun" as a discovery sign.[43] In addition to talking on the phone, the "girls" walk together in a choreographed line, moving to the beat of the music arm in arm, symbolizing their take-back of the street.[44] The choreography is positively charged because it reinforces, and is reinforced by, the lyrical content and visual imagery.

Dance, then, can be interpreted here as a marginalized activity that dis-tinguishes black and female performers from white men. Dance is also a powerful, empowering action, sometimes in the form of access or discov-ery signs. Returning to the present data, we find evident that the percent-ages presented above cannot illuminate to what extent these individuals (blacks, women) are empowered or disempowered by dance. They do not point to, for instance, *who* performs the choreography. While an in-depth look at all of the videos to examine who performs within which style is ex-cessive and cumbersome, it is useful to choose the most frequently aired choreographed videos from the sample to examine how choreographed dance functions within them. Accordingly, table 4.2 identifies these videos.

The most popular video featuring a white female for both stations the week of my sample was Mariah Carey's "Fantasy."[45] Directed by Carey, this video was also the number one video on the *MTV Jams Countdown* that week (*MTV Jams* was a popular morning show on MTV during the time of the sample). The narrative depicts the singer rollerblading and enjoying the rides at an amusement park during the day. When nighttime falls, in the second verse, Carey sings and dances while on top of a jeep; in front of her a group of male dancers perform a choreographed routine (all the men are black with the exception of one white male). The most frequently played video featuring a white female artist on both stations, then, features hired, primarily black male dancers but does not involve the artist herself, other than in some lower-level movement while she sings.

The only other example of black men dancing is in Silk's "Hooked On You," the most frequently aired video to feature black males on MuchMusic.

Table 4.2

The Most Frequently Aired Choreographed Videos Featuring White Men, White Women, Black Men, and Black Women on MTV and MuchMusic

MTV	
White female artist	Mariah Carey, "Fantasy"
Black female artist	Salt-N-Pepa, "Ain't Nuthin' But a She Thing"
White male artist	Chris Isaak, "Go Walking down There"
Black male artist	R. Kelly, "You Remind Me of Something"
MuchMusic	
White female artist	Mariah Carey, "Fantasy"
Black female artist	Janet Jackson, "Runaway"
White male artist	Bryan Adams, "Have You Ever Really Loved a Woman?"
Black male artist	Silk, "Hooked on You"

In "Hooked," the urban vocal group sings in a hotel to three onlooking women. While the singers perform, the seemingly innocent women slip out and rob the hotel's safe. A series of short clips show the vocal group briefly dancing a choreographed routine in silhouette.

R. Kelly's "You Remind Me Of Something," the most frequently aired choreographed video featuring a black male on MTV, features the artist performing for an audience at a nighttime "Jeep-Nik Jam."[46] Like Mariah Carey's video, the artist moves while he sings, but others (in this case, three unknown black female dancers) perform the choreographed dancing. These three women are dressed in basketball sweatshirts, appear on cement with courtlike white markings, and move suggestively with basketballs. The dancers, however, are never shot together with Kelly. Instead, they are at best peripheral to the artist, present when seen but forgotten when out of the camera frame.

Similarly, Chris Isaak's "Go Walking Down There," MTV's most played choreographed video featuring a white male, does not involve the performer in the choreographed dance. In this video, Isaak acts within a narrative lamenting the loss of his beloved, and also performs in a room with orange paint and 1960s oversized flowers decorating the walls. In this same space, white male and female youths dance to the text "look at all you happy people . . . look at all your smiling faces." These youths are dressed in bathing suits and appear almost psychotically happy, contrasting with Isaak's despondent disposition. Like R. Kelly's video, the artist never dances, nor does he ever share the same visual frame with the dancers.

MTV's most popular video featuring a black female artist was Salt-N-Pepa's articulation of African American hip-hop in "Ain't Nuthin' But a

She Thing."[47] "Ain't Nuthin' But a She Thing," unlike the videos previously described, features the artists performing an American-derived dance style. This video incorporates both access and discovery signs. The text refers to women taking control ("fight for your right, stand up and be heard / you're just as good as any man") and the images are of women in nontraditional roles, as firefighters, astronauts, and police officers. The dance is performed in a gymlike setting with the three primary artists up front and a group of women, both black and white, mirroring them in a militaristic style. Periodically, the artists also join them to dance alongside in solidarity. Dance functions, like the narrative, as an access sign. Through both the taking-back of a traditionally male-dominated area (the military) and their sharp technique, the women demonstrate their technical proficiency within this realm.

Of these videos, only two ("Hooked on You" and "Ain't Nuthin' but a She Thing") involve the featured artists as choreographed dancers. The primary artists in each of these videos were either black males or black females—corroborating what was suggested previously, that marginalized demographic groups are featured more often as dancers. Once again, black women, arguably the most marginalized of the demographic groups, were featured most often. These videos could also be seen to reinforce particular racial identities within the United States and Canada. Salt-N-Pepa's video, for instance, incorporates rap (a commonly perceived "American genre," particularly for Americans), hip-hop dance (another indigenous American movement lexicon), and images of narratives in American diners and on American streets. These incorporations, in combination with the significant alignment of the rap repertoire on the station, reinforce the perception of a segment of black American popular culture artists unambiguously situated within the American nation-state.

On MuchMusic, meanwhile, other patterns were developing within the video repertoire. MuchMusic's most frequently aired video featuring a female black artist was Janet Jackson's "Runaway."[48] "Runaway" was shown twenty-two times that week on MuchMusic, almost double the number of airings on MTV—a highly unusual practice for an American video. Popular Canadian videos tend to receive substantial airtime on MuchMusic to meet the Canadian content quota, but videos featuring American celebrities like Jackson usually receive considerably more airtime on MTV than MuchMusic. In "Runaway," Jackson travels the world by physically "jumping" between locations (New York, Sydney, Rio, Paris) to the text "I've seen the world, been to many places / made lots of friends, many different races." Her dress and jewelry are a combination of non-Western styles; she wears extensive makeup, appears with her hair up and "exotically" straightened and her eyeglasses diagonally pointed. This constructed image, it quickly becomes evident, allows Jackson to fit in visually with the other non-Western dancers. The choreographed sequence, set on the Leaning Tower of Pisa and on a seemingly moving airplane wing, features her and the other female dancers performing in a South Asian style. As the text suggests, she's traveling worldwide and sampling cultures: "I woke up with an Australian breeze, and danced the dance with Aborigines."

Because Jackson and the other women clearly enjoy dancing as a positive expression, this component might qualify as one of Lewis's "discovery" signs. But "Runaway" also raises questions about discovery signs and their *cross-cultural* appropriation. This dance may be a "female activity," but, significantly, not indigenous for Jackson. Within the context of the video this tradition is something appropriated on the whirlwind, worldwide tour. The women (allegedly those who actually perform it) give Jackson credibility, but remain nameless.[49] It is difficult, then, to label the use of dance within this video as a "discovery" sign; to do so is to assume that the performers are empowered by the choreography, which is not the case. Instead, these women fall within what Toni Morrison has called an "economy of stereotype," whereby the author of the text invents a "quick and easy image without the responsibility of specificity [or] accuracy."[50] Spanish guitar music used to represent Mexicans or acoustic instruments used to signify women within movie soundtracks are but two examples of these easy stereotypes. Only Jackson is empowered by borrowing (other) women's tradition, rendering this act more of a cross-cultural access sign than a feminist discovery sign.

"Runaway" undoubtedly was designed for viewing on American MTV. The designers likely made certain assumptions about the "preferred" decoding strategies of the American viewing audience (after all, Michael Jackson's "Black or White" proved a huge success on MTV and "Runaway" resembles this video's appropriative style). But what about MTV's international stations? Are the representational politics of this video more charged when it is aired on stations like MTV Europe or MTV Asia? What are the repercussions of seeing a non-Western expression that is unproblematically absorbed into Western aesthetics, and then "reflected" back in altered form to the culture of origin? Is this of concern to MTV? In a word, yes. Unproblematic, free-flowing cultural articulations are at the core of MTV's transnational agenda. "In the past decade," William Sonnega notes, "few forms of media have more relentlessly capitalized on simulations . . . than . . . MTV, in which the world's diverse peoples, cultures, and most emphatically "colors" are conflated in utopian technological scenarios."[51] Nowhere is this conflating more obvious than in Michael Jackson's "Black or White," in which morphing is used to facilitate racial/ethnic flow within the cultural "melting pot." This video is an example of what Sonnega describes as the deeply set North American or European multicultural models that are simply unattainable "melting pot" ideals.[52] ("Runaway" does not celebrate cultural diversity so much as represent multiculturalist modes of stereotypical economy.) As Sonnega further notes, "the driving force behind MTV's multicultural makeover was the fact that the channel is broadcast in 137 nations . . . to maintain profitability, MTV was forced to expand its gaze to include representations . . . of peoples and cultures outside those its demographic consultants had 'targeted' as profitable."[53] In marketing to this broad range of countries, MTV must avoid critical analysis of the conflicts that affect the everyday lives of its viewers.[54] "Runaway" typifies this style. It is a representation of seemingly "friendly" intercultural exchange, evidence to other countries of MTV's cultural openness.

That openness may be part of the rationale behind "Runaway"'s original design and its subsequent use by MTV, but I am talking about a slightly different context here. Canadian audiences watching MuchMusic, for instance, might read this video differently. Given the intensity with which this video was aired on the station, it could contribute toward a viewer's perception of openness toward non-Western influences—perhaps MuchMusic's self-proclaimed celebration of multicultural exchange as part of a uniquely *Canadian* agenda.

While it is very difficult to attribute anything to the heavy rotation of only one video, a pattern arises when we view "Runaway" alongside MuchMusic's most frequently aired choreographed video featuring a white male: Bryan Adams's "Have You Ever Really Loved A Woman?" from the movie *Don Juan de Marco*. (This video was not shown once on MTV during the sampled week.) "Have You Ever," like "Runaway," is ripe for a critical analysis of cultural appropriation but I would like instead to examine this video for the ways in which difference is negotiated. Whereas Janet Jackson transformed physically and stylistically to blend in with the dancers (and thereby legitimate her claim to their cultural traditions), Adams's participation is more complex. Here I highlight his initial difference from, and partial admittance into, the world of the "ethnic other" vis-à-vis the use of light.

For this analysis I borrow from Richard Dyer's 1997 book *White*.[55] In this text, Dyer presents a compelling analysis of the social construction of whiteness from classical painting to contemporary Hollywood movies. What links his wide-ranging texts is the way in which whiteness is perpetuated as both normative, and as the site of social, political, and cultural dominance. Of particular interest for my work here is his analysis of the use of light to accentuate whiteness. He states: "Light is a defining term . . . how different groups relate to it profoundly affects their place in society." As he argues further, within the realm of hegemonic Western representation: "Those who can let the light through . . . whose bodies are touched by the light from above, who yearn upward towards it, those are the people who should rule and inherit the earth." From the latter half of the second decade of the twentieth century on, ideal movie lighting was referred to as "Northern" light—soft, white, and steeply slanted. "The North, in ethnocentric geography, in the map of the world that became standardized in the process of European expansion, is above the South." Northern light, therefore, is "literally and symbolically, superior light." Within the realm of theater and cinema, Dyer writes, overhead and backlighting inject this type of light, which not only ensures that the actor is separated from the background, but that "the ethnically loaded evils of shadow . . . can be eliminated."[56]

Before I examine Adams's video "Have You Ever Really Loved a Woman?" I shall briefly contextualize my analysis through another Adams video from the MuchMusic sample that preceded "Have You Ever Really Loved A Woman?" on several occasions that week. "Everything I Do, I Do It For You,"[57] from the soundtrack *Robin Hood, Prince of Thieves,* was a huge song for Adams in 1991, charting at number one for seven weeks in the United States and twelve weeks in Canada. In Britain, "Everything I Do" enjoyed the most consecutive weeks at number one on the U.K. Top 40 charts to that date.[58] This immensely popular song/video saturated radio and video stations alike across North America and Western Europe. Its appearance before "Have You Ever Really Loved A Woman?" in 1995, then, certainly drew many viewers to their television sets.

The use of light is significant in this video. In particular, Adams alone seems to attract the soft Northern rays. The musical performance is set in a forest intercut with clips from the movie. When the band is shown, the rays appear on Adams's face and over his shoulder. Occasionally the light's glare is so powerful that the image is indecipherable. At the opening to the next video, "Have You Ever Really Loved A Woman?[59] Adams walks into a dark bar filled with the locals and their "ethnic" shadows, leaving behind the strong, outdoor light. As light continues to pour in from outside the doorway, Adams, dressed in white, sings as if to "enlighten" those still "in the dark." But the doorway is not the only source of light. At times, light seems to emanate from Adams himself, particularly when he is in the company of the video's unidentified, undifferentiated women. During the guitar solo, Adams alone moves closer to a second source of external light, a hanging light bulb. Adams stands on top of a table close to the light while the featured guitar soloist, Paco de Lucia, performs relatively unnoticed from floor level. This positioning renders Adams's elevation incongruent with his musically less important role of strumming the accompaniment chords but congruent with his inherited access to the symbolic power of this important light source.

This new source, however, is unable to eliminate the dangerous shadows that mark the outdoor nighttime dance sequence that ends the video. This scene is marked by a plethora of long shadows cast by the dancers on a background wall. Adams, because of his close proximity to the wall, casts a very short shadow, while de Lucia, who sits and plays in the foreground, casts an elongated and darkened shadow (thanks to the use of floor lighting). The female dancers' shadows, not surprisingly, are the longest and most threatening of all. Never is Adams's whiteness threatened or tainted.

These two "ethnically inflected" videos aired with frequency on Much-Music, although neither video qualified as "Canadian content." "Runaway" is American-made and too many parameters of "Have You Ever Really Loved A Woman?" were produced outside of Canada to label it a "domestic" product here.[60] Their frequency on MuchMusic, then, did nothing to further the stations' Canadian content quota. Weaving these images into a heavy rotation, however, could reflect MuchMusic's attempt to target a particularly Canadian audience within the context of Canada's multicultural imaginary. Lucy Lippard's observations are informative in light of these two videos and their rotational frequency on MuchMusic: "The dominant culture prefers to make over its sources into its own image, filtering them through the sieve of recent local art history, seeing only that which is familiar or currently marketable and rejecting that which cannot be squeezed into 'our' framework."[61] It is precisely because of Adams's and Jackson's familiar personas to Canadian viewers that non-Western images (and in particular non-Western dance) can be successfully "squeezed" into their videos and function as part of a contained multicultural imagination.

I would argue that these videos served another purpose. Their heavy rotation pleased shareholders through the inclusion of mainstream performers while, intentionally or not, they simultaneously furthered the station's multicultural rhetoric. If MuchMusic could implement such CRTC imperatives as the mosaic rubric—thanks in part to a complex multicultural rhetoric, as I have suggested here—MTV's designs for entrance into the Canadian marketplace would be rejected. I wonder, then, if there is a slight irony embedded here. If MTV's corporate, multinational agenda encouraged the production of videos that promoted cultural diversity for foreign consumption, and stations like MuchMusic aired these same videos in a heavy rotation, MTV's own initiatives could have prevented them from expanding into the market right next door.

Perhaps. But the reasons MTV may never fully reach into Canada extend beyond governmental policy. The multicultural narratives that pervaded

Canadian cultural discourses in 1995—and continue to do so today—were distinct, complex, and contradictory, and MuchMusic saw itself as a forum through which these narratives could be heard. Like any other station, MuchMusic had systemic modes of multiracial containment. For instance, in 1995 the number of videos featuring African Americans on both stations was significantly increased over the previous decade; simultaneously, however, there was a shift to featuring fewer politically oppositional videos on MTV and more black female performers in highly sexualized, choreographed dance styles (especially on MuchMusic). But these modes were challenged daily on MuchMusic by videos featuring artists like the Dream Warriors, who spoke for many Canadians by activating the local, embracing the global, and by problematizing their place within that continuum. These modes were also contested by MuchMusic's expanded and historically deeper video repertoire, which allowed space for socially oppositional videos (such as those discussed here from the African diaspora). This rich, hybrid space of the "in between" was where Canadian youth carved out a piece of their identity—not despite but *because* of the contradictions and tensions they inherited, while successfully perpetuating the station's continued instability and perpetual renewal.

CHAPTER FIVE

MuchMusic and MTV
The Finnish Context

Within the limited MuchMusic scholarly literature most attention has fo-cused on the domestic station and less on its international stations and pro-grams. These exports sometimes have been dismissed as culturally unprob-lematic. Such was the case with MuchUSA (1994–2000), which took its content directly from MuchMusic with American-tailored programs occa-sionally inserted into the schedule.[1] The issues surrounding another inter-national collaboration, Finland's *Jyrki,* an after-school music video pro-gram modeled after MuchMusic and aired on Finland's largest commercial television station MTV3 (no relation to MTV), were considerably more complex because the program combined North American and Finnish popular culture. This content raised questions surrounding the show's pro-gramming: were Finns watching primarily North American performers or a balance of Finnish and international artists? To what extent did Finnish musicians have to adapt to North American video styles to receive airplay? From the moment the after-school program was launched on September 1, 1995, English and Finnish flowed at *Jyrki's* bilingual Helsinki streetfront lo-cation while the videos played (also in both languages), frequently inter-rupted by the logos of affluent international advertisers eager to buy com-mercial time. Viewer response initially was tremendous, prompting local Finnish competitors to imitate *Jyrki's* innovative new format. Indeed, the program was so successful that television executives described it as the sty-listic protocol for Finland's future digital television format.

When *Jyrki* premiered in 1995, MTV Nordic dominated Finnish music television. While Finnish music industry insiders described MTV as the most important and influential video station of the first half of the 1990s, viewers increasingly described it as distant and inaccessible, a sentiment that became more pronounced after *Jyrki's* debut. This perception was due in part to MTV's distant recording location (London) and its low Nordic video content, the combination of which starkly contrasted with *Jyrki*'s video repertoire, which included more Finnish acts, and regional inflections. *Jyrki* entered the market to reclaim the local and make a stronger connection between viewers and the station. *Jyrki*, like MuchMusic, strove to present itself as a local service by taping and reporting "live" from a busy streetfront with an exposed working environment, openly displaying the cameras, production crews, and people on the street, who were shown through the building's large windows. But the competition did not end there: in 1999, another local station, Moon TV, launched a handful of music video programs targeting what they perceived to be demographic gaps in *Jyrki* and MTV Nordic's programming; it quickly built a loyal following of artists and viewers. By 2000, then, there were three stations/programs actively competing for music video viewers in the small country of Finland.

In this chapter I turn from the domestic stations to explore how *Jyrki*/ MuchMusic competed with MTV in Finland and how their efforts changed Finns' relationship not only to popular music but also to their local and global geographical environments. This work draws upon three fieldwork trips to Finland (2000, 2001, and 2003) during which time I conducted interviews with executives from television and radio stations as well as their local competitors, representatives from Finnish music funding sources, industry marketers, video directors, musicians, Finnish media academics, and, most important, music television viewers. These viewers were university students and several faculty members from two southern Finnish cities, Helsinki and Turku (twelve respondents in Helsinki, and seventeen in Turku). I chose to interview respondents from Helsinki because it is Finland's largest city with almost a half-million people and also the home of *Jyrki*. Turku, an older city west of Helsinki with a population of approximately 170,000 people and the fourth-largest Finnish city, was chosen because of its smaller size and close proximity to the larger capital. This interview process included group interviews and written questionnaires (please see appendix B). My respondents were studying music, although not necessarily as majors, at the University of Helsinki, Turku University, and the Swedish Academy in Turku; their ages, with only a few exceptions, ranged from eighteen to twenty-four. Many of these individuals watched *Jyrki* when it began in 1995. At that time they would have been between the ages of twelve and eighteen, a target demographic for the station.

This chapter diverges methodologically from the first four chapters in which I executed a content analysis of MuchMusic's and MTV's North American stations. This quantitative approach was useful for these chapters because I was interested in exploring questions surrounding differences in the stations' content as opposed to how diverse audiences read these texts. As a North American insider who had engaged in lengthy discussions with MuchMusic and MTV viewers (two demographics without much overlap), I wanted to see if my current findings corroborated or refuted commonly held perceptions. Once this research was completed and I better understood the domestic stations' content from the sampled week, I was interested in exploring MuchMusic's and MTV's impact beyond the North American border. There were several international locations where the stations were in competition and were influencing local media practices, including Argentina and Finland. As a cultural outsider, I required access to local viewers so they could help me decode the stations' contents; this qualitative approach would help me avoid misreading locally inflected texts.

It is in part for this reason that I chose Finland as the site of my study. Through Finnish academic colleagues I had access to a range of informants with whom I could conduct group interviews and individual written questionnaires. I also chose Finland because possible parallels could be drawn between the cultural and small market economies of Finland and Canada. Both countries struggle to gain cultural recognition, eclipsed by their powerful neighbors, Sweden and the United States, who dominate Scandinavian and North American popular culture respectively. Both countries also negotiate two official languages—English and French in Canada, and Finnish and Swedish in Finland—and in both countries multilinguistic inclusion simultaneously enriches and destabilizes uniform national identities. Additional unique Finnish features that make it an advantageous ethnographic site will be discussed shortly.

That I began my fieldwork in Finland five years after the North American sample was taken initially might seem problematic. This is a significant time gap, perhaps too significant for this material to be tied to the preceeding chapters. Because it takes a number of years for media outlets to establish their style and cultural influence, however, it was important to give *Jyrki*, which began broadcasting in 1995, sufficient time before a carefully considered analysis could be conducted. Accordingly, the time gap between the sample dates and the onset of fieldwork, while significant, was also a necessity.

For all of the above reasons, this chapter stands alone. It begins as a case study of how media outlets move beyond nation-state borders and struggle with the question that faces many other international companies: how is it possible to become locally relevant to viewers while maintaining an internationally recognized brand and spread a fairly homogenous (and cost-effective) snapshot of Western culture? Sometimes this task necessitates an alteration of the brand itself. In fact, I shall show through this analysis that MuchMusic's mandate of local specificity, will have different, and sometimes contradictory effects when executed abroad. While this mandate is certainly not one of the Canadian cultural narratives explored in the previous chapters, it is critical to the Citytv/Muchmusic brand. Canadians, upon hearing that the MuchMusic format is exported, might assume that the station serves other cities as it does theirs, that is, by showcasing local artists and videos, and by accentuating domestic specificity. In the pages that follow I argue that the MuchMusic known to millions of Canadian youth has not been neatly replicated in Finland, and, in fact, the adapted format can result in the loss of "the local." Not only has this newly assimilated format changed the way Finnish youth write, produce, and consume music television; it has, in fact, altered the global landscapes within which they live.

Why Finland?

In addition to access to informants and Canadian/Finnish parallels, Finland provides a unique context within which to explore the tensions between global and local media. First, the country is an international leader in communications technologies. Finland perhaps is best known as the home of Nokia, the world's largest mobile phone company (and, as of 2006, the fifth most recognized brand name globally). Nokia's importance to Finland's economy is significant: in 2001 the company was responsible for 15 percent of Finnish exports and up to half of the country's gross domestic product.[2] And Finns are eager telecommunication participants: by the close of 2005 there were 5.38 million cell phone subscribers, that is, 103 percent of the Finnish population.[3] Moreover, Finns are heavy Internet users: by the end of 2005, Finland had more than 1.3 million Internet connections, which is approximately 250 per 1,000 citizens.[4] Technology-based firms including Hewlett-Packard and IBM have set up testing laboratories there, recognizing that this northern corner of Europe, with its relatively small and homogeneous population, is an exceptional testing ground for new technologies. In short, Finns are open to learning and experimenting with new communications technologies and styles, creating a unique opportunity to explore the effects of global media expansions.

Finns are also unique because of their very strong language skills: the majority of Finnish adults have at least ten years of English study in school.[5] As mentioned previously, Finland, like Canada, is an officially bilingual country; all Finns study Swedish in school and the vast majority of Swedish-speaking Finns (6 percent of the overall population) reside in the southern regions. A defining feature of Finnish television is that foreign-language programs are never dubbed into Finnish (with the exception of some commercials and children's programs), which means that Finns, more so than many other European citizens and North Americans, are exposed to foreign languages as they are actually spoken.[6] As a result, many Finns have a comfort level in a number of foreign languages including German, Swedish, Russian, and particularly English. Moreover, many private and state-owned firms pay for students to complete upper-level graduate work abroad, particularly in England and the United States. The Finns' ability to understand and eagerness to consume English-language—and especially American—television programming, combined with their advances in communications technologies have prompted analysts to nickname Finland the most American of European countries.[7]

However, unlike the United States, Finland has a small music industry that is relatively less musically defined. This smallness may have contributed to its appeal as a market in which to expand where a local music television program could play an important role in the development of domestic music, and music video styles. Until only recently, Finland has had difficulty identifying a unique style, in part because it suffered from a little-brother complex with regard to its next-door neighbor, Sweden, which has long dominated the Scandinavian market.[8] To illustrate this point, consider the following statistic: In 1998, Sweden's music exports were valued at 1.5 billion Finnish marks (1 FIM = $.20 in U.S. dollars), while Finland's exports totaled only about 50 million FIMs. Sweden, of course, was placed on the map in 1974 when Abba won the Eurovision Song contest and music subsequently became Sweden's third-largest export. Finland has long been frustrated at this contest, placing last a record-breaking seven times, occasionally with no points whatsoever. Reasons for this failure elude most, although Finnish musicians have been accused of being behind current trends. This backwardness has changed over the past few years and groups like love metal band HIM and electro/hip-hop/funk band Bomfunk MC have made a mark internationally, thanks in part to *Jyrki*'s Finnish presence. So, while it was Finnish television executives who initially made inquiries to MuchMusic about the possibility of acquiring a franchise, by 1995 the parent Canadian company found the prospect exciting. Even today Finland provides an exceptional opportunity for researchers to examine MuchMusic's international influence.[9]

Finnish Television

There are four national broadcast television channels in Finland, including two public service channels (YLE 1 and YLE 2) and two commercial channels

(TV4 [Nelonen] and MTV3). In 2000, a typical evening's programming on the commercial stations included a combination of old and new North American programming including episodes of *Dynasty, Baywatch,* and *Seinfeld,* as well as Hollywood-made movies. As elsewhere in Europe, all four stations are in contact with a growing number of cable and satellite services; because these services are still fairly limited relative to the number of subscribers who receive public services, the public stations still dominate Finnish television airwaves. In Finland, cable and satellite offer programming mainly in foreign languages (German, Danish, Russian, and English), and the most popular channels include NBC Europe, France's TV5, Europsport and MTV Nordic.[10] Half of Finnish households who now have cable can watch the NBC Nightly News, Germany's RTL, Spain's TVE, Italy's Raiuno, Moscow Channel 1 (all commercial channels), and French and Swedish public service, as well as the BBC. Digital terrestrial and cable transmissions began in Finland in 2001, and, as the country continues to move quickly toward digital broadcasting, analog broadcasts are scheduled to end in 2007. Finland will then be the first country to have moved completely into a digital format.

MTV's Entry into Finland

How to manage global markets has been a challenge for many international businesses and MTV has not been exempt from this issue. The network began exporting in 1984 when a station in Australia broadcasted five hours of MTV under license; that same year, MTV Japan was launched. MTV clearly began their international enterprises with the attitude of trying to develop one single market with a unified image. As MTV Chair Tom Freston explained, "From the outset, our vision has been that this would be a worldwide rock-and-roll network."[11] Indeed, MTV attempted to structure its exports as a limited number of broad-ranging markets instead of more customized regions. In August 1997, MTV Europe was launched in fourteen European countries, the format of which resembled that of the American station. According to a 1991 study of the station's playlist only about 15 percent of the artists were European.[12] MTV programmers, meanwhile, attempted to make the Japanese station appear more local by using Japanese hosts and artists while nonetheless maintaining an American style. They were unsuccessful and MTV programming went off the air in Japan in 1991 as local imitators, playing more indigenous acts, proved more successful.[13] The following year a station entitled Music Channel was established and received the Japanese rights to the American version of MTV.[14]

MTV's global expansion continued at an impressive rate; by 1996 the network was reported to reach 260 million households in seventy countries. By then, however, smaller stations were building audiences by using local talent and singing in indigenous languages. MTV responded to their competition by customizing their services further. MTV Europe, for instance, split into a cluster of regional markets creating a series of European MTV-branded services including MTV Southern (Italy), Central (Germany/Switzerland/Austria), U.K., and Ireland, among others. MTV Nordic became the Scandinavian offering, combining the MTV Europe feed with one half-hour program called *Nordic Top 5*. Like MTV Europe, this program featured a VJ who introduced the top five Nordic videos in English from a decontextualized London studio.

This regional station, like all of the others, attempted to reflect local interests. For instance, MTV Nordic implemented a "person placement" technique: programs like *Total Request,* for instance, featured videos introduced by people on the street who dedicate the song to friends, family, or lovers. Stefan in Sweden, for example, might have dedicated a video to Dorit in Israel. Dedications were also shown at the bottom of the screen during segments of the show, adding to a more personalized aura. Finally, MTV created the impression of pan-European participation vis-à-vis the video's introduction. Before some of the videos were shown, the text "Made in (name of country)" flashed across the screen with the image of a world map in the background. "Made in Belgium" or "Made in Finland," then, gave the impression of a balanced power dynamic between, and more equal participation of, European countries.

MuchMusic's Entry into Finland

With increased competition from new cable channels and a desire to introduce an alternative music video format to MTV Nordic, MTV3 decided in 1994 that it was important to draw a younger audience. Executive Marko Kulmala (later executive producer of *Jyrki*) was collaborating on a proposal for a new, younger station image when they "stumbled" into Citytv, a privately owned television system owned by CHUM Limited.[15] The Citytv brand, founded in 1972, featured a new approach to journalism; the technology was intentionally displayed, cameras were usually handheld, and the format was more informal (this format is also that adopted for MuchMusic). Finnish representatives subsequently traveled to Toronto to study the possibility of a joint project with Citytv. The agreement was a part production, supply, licensing, and formal arrangement; the rights included the use of MuchMusic's name, production consultation and access to staff training.

Once the specifics were agreed upon, *Jyrki* was launched on MTV3 and was immediately available to 4.8 million households. In 2000, Citytv's brand expansion continued with a station called TVTV! that aired material from the numerous Citytv stations (Space, StarTV, and others), American and British programming as well as in-house Citytv produced programs (*Media Television*).[16] The MuchMusic/Jyrki format then, was only Citytv's first step into Finland. The Canadian network then began providing programming for two of the most popular commercial Finnish television stations. Their emphasis on Finland rather than the pan-European scene, they hoped, would entice Finnish viewers to turn away from MTV Nordic and move toward Helsinki and Finnish popular culture.

How well did *Jyrki*'s and MTV Nordic's regionalizing strategies work? Did the notion of Nordicity resonate with Finnish viewers so as to make them feel "at home" while watching MTV Nordic? Or did *Jyrki*'s regional emphasis prove more successful?

As part of my fieldwork I asked my Finnish informants whether or not they felt a sense of regionality living in a northern country. Through the interviews it became apparent that most of my informants indeed identified as "Nordic." Eighteen of the twenty-six informants who responded to the question felt a sense of Nordicity for a number of reasons, ranging from shared Scandinavian social policies (especially education and health care), to shared languages, history, and culture. Such was particularly true with Swedish-speaking Finns, who felt they could communicate more easily with other Scandinavians because of the close geographical connection between Sweden and Finland. Indeed, this connection might allow some to identify as "Nordic" rather than exclusively Swedish or Finnish, as well as engender a closer relationship between Swedish and the other Nordic languages (Finnish is the most distant of the Scandinavian languages). Despite the connections my informants felt with Nordicity, however, only few of them felt that MTV Nordic supported or reified a sense of Nordicity for them individually. Most responded that it created a sense of place from elsewhere ("They [only create] a sense of America"; or, "It creates the sense of an international people"). Only a few felt that there was a sense of Nordicity ("probably, especially among youngsters . . . I think there are VJs from different countries"). The overall negative response was not surprising; with just one half-hour Nordic-specific show produced in London, there was too little contact with local articulations to be "local." This was an instance of MTV's wanting a sense of regionality, but not being willing to support the local level necessary to feel familiar to viewers.

Olli Oikarinen, former *Jyrki* editor-in-chief, explained that by the mid-1990s, MTV Nordic was perceived to be more distant and less Finnish.

Like the American station, MTV Nordic communicated a sense of urgency and speed by counting down the seconds to the next music video in the corner of the television screen. *Jyrki*, however, did not count down to videos and, with the extended VJ commentary, the program appeared to have a slower pace. Because *Jyrki* also provided Finnish subtitles for their foreign content (as did other Finnish programs), it appeared to be even more local (MTV did not subtitle). As a result, *Jyrki* proved far more accessible when it debuted—so much so, Oikarinen explained, that the viewers felt as if they could "touch it." My viewer informants agreed, stating that *Jyrki* had a slower tempo, reflecting a more Finnish sensibility. My informants also noted that because the VJs were Finns, they could be more personal with the audience and more relaxed as they spoke about local issues and interests.

The resemblance between *Jyrki* and Toronto's MuchMusic was significant from the outset, although *Jyrki* executives would discourage too close a comparison. Promotions executive Kristiina Werner, who trained in Toronto at MuchMusic, felt that the magazine format of the Finnish product was slower than the flow at MuchMusic and that the Finnish VJs told longer stories and talked at a slower pace.[17] Most executives with whom I spoke also reported that because Finland is more open to explicit sexual content on television, *Jyrki* was more liberal than the Canadian station in their choice of videos, creating a substantially different energy from the parent station. Whereas the stylistic and content differences between MuchMusic and *Jyrki* may not have seemed overly pronounced to the untrained eye, the physical resemblance between the two environments—from the colors of the walls and floors, to the open concept and exposed technology, to the use of logos—was striking. As one viewer informant stated: "It's only the language that changes. [Otherwise] it's the same."

This consistency raised questions around how closely the younger program had to follow the MuchMusic protocol and how much room there was for local inflections. I posed this question to Marco Bresba, a representative from CHUM Limited in Toronto (owners of Citytv) who was in Helsinki for the summer of 2000 to help the station "brush up" on the MuchMusic technique. Bresba explained that there was considerable space for local inflections at *Jyrki*. MuchMusic, he explained, doesn't hold the mirror asking the Finns to reflect their format; rather, they "show them how to hold the mirror to properly reflect what is going on locally." He used Finland's version of *Speaker's Corner* as an example of how the local was injected. In Canada, this program airs on Citytv's local Toronto station and is composed of footage of people coming into a booth and expressing opinions on current issues. This material then is edited and thematically grouped for airplay. In the Finnish version of the show, participants type in their messages on their cell phone and, for five marks, watch their message scroll on the television screen. On weekdays there is no host; on the weekends there is a host who responds to the text messages verbally, but the television personality's persona is not developed, creating a limited connection between the viewer and host. In other words, viewers are watching for the messages themselves and less for the connection with the show's host. This program has been very popular among Finns: in 2000 it received on average between five and six thousand hits a night. Bresba saw this practice of typing *Speaker's Corner* messages as very Finnish for two reasons. The first is technological, reflecting the Finnish enthusiasm for text-based messaging discussed previously. The second reason is cultural: Finns are discursively constructed as shyer and less talkative than their European peers. This format, then, seemed to befit their interactive styles perfectly, making *Speaker's Corner* (significantly *without* a corner, a point to which I shall return momentarily) an effective Finnish adaptation of a Canadian concept.

When *Jyrki, Speaker's Corner,* and the other Citytv shows were launched in Finland, there was an eager viewer response to the adapted programs. Subsequently, there were increasing grievances made against the programs, including one significant criticism directed against *Jyrki* that echoed that made against MuchMusic. Helsinki, like Toronto, was accused of being too often the focal point of the program. As my informants from Turku responded, this disproportion has resulted in the marginalization of various local music scenes. In Finland, this problem is significant—the country is famous for its summer music festivals in the smaller cities including Turku, Tampere, and other outlying areas where local musicians are featured. These festivals include Ruisrock—the oldest Finnish rock festival held in Ruissalo on the outskirts of Turku—and the Pori Jazz Festival on the west coast of the country, among many others. According to my viewer informants, *Jyrki* has been less in contact with these music scenes. Again, *Jyrki* executives would disagree. Olli Oikarinen explained that the program had made tremendous efforts to reach the outlying areas with tours to six Finnish cities. Kristiina Werner reiterated *Jyrki*'s commitment to reaching distant viewers, noting that twice a year *Jyrki* goes out on tour to every major city in Finland for two months. That these tours reached cities rather than smaller towns is an important distinction for my informants. I shall return to this point shortly.

A second complaint made against *Jyrki* by Finnish musicians and video directors was the pressure to sing in English in order to facilitate access into the "international repertoire" (which is also an issue for MTV Nordic).

Whether or not to perform in English is a crucial question for non-English musicians. As Harris M. Berger has noted, language choice affects everything from the lyrical inflection to the size of a recording contract, and musicians must ask what it means to sing in any language, be that native, foreign, colonial, or their own.[18] The perception among most interviewees—viewers, performers and video directors—was that *Jyrki* shifted its original focus from including more of the edgier local musics sung in Finnish to featuring more of the safer international English repertoire. Thus many Finns were sidelined, especially those who began recording in Finnish hoping they would receive airplay on the station. In 2000, Oikarinen estimated that approximately 20 percent of all videos shown on *Jyrki* were in Finnish while 80 percent were in English.[19] Nonetheless, viewer perception was that Finnish videos were increasingly less welcome on the station and that between 1995 and 2000, *Jyrki* increasingly resembled MTV Nordic.

The perception that *Jyrki* began to mirror its larger competitor vis-à-vis the international video repertoire created space for another video source, and in late 1999 a small yet feisty competitor called Moon TV joined MTV Nordic and *Jyrki*. From the outset this station featured specialized programs like *666 Seconds* for harder-alternative musics and *Bubblegum* for pop music fans. According to Elli Suvaninen, Moon TV executive and programmer, the station tried to show one Finnish video for every two in English in order to keep the local emphasis.[20] Moon TV was also active on the Finnish Festival Circuit, often using an interviewer and a single camera, communicating a more cutting-edge, low-production image. Within a year of its launch, Moon TV had become the most "local" Finnish media outlet, bringing both major urban centers and smaller communities together and playing Finnish videos with more violent and sexual content that would not have been seen on the other stations. By 2000, video directors and musicians saw this station as the emerging, critical music video outlet, particularly for newly breaking acts.

Although *Jyrki* was the show that first attempted to reflect Finnish popular culture back to its viewers, it seemed to lose its edge after Moon TV's debut. Admittedly, *Jyrki* had more externally imposed limitations than MTV Nordic or Moon TV from the outset. Because it aired in the postschool timeslot (3:30–5:00 P.M. weekdays), it had a significant young audience and certain themes could not be shown owing to television standard laws. Certain musics, of course, were also important to draw desirable sponsors. Such pressures formed the repertoire from the outset and continued to shape it as the program matured.

According to my informants, *Jyrki* also changed its focus to include more foreign English-language videos, the repercussions of which did more than change the video lineup aired on television. As *Jyrki* drew from more international sources and Citytv increased its presence in Finland, the actual connection Finns have with their own country also was reshaped. The musics and musicians heard on the station that began as locally inflected increasingly became more international and urban-based, marginalizing performers from the smaller outlying Finnish communities. Rather than strengthening connections with the Finnish rural areas (where the previously cited popular music festivals take place), my informants noted that *Jyrki* instead began to privilege non-Finnish, urban-based material. As I began to examine these relationships to other localities it was apparent that the connections were not only to other countries but to particular urban centers, including Toronto, New York, Montreal, and London. This connectivity was immediately apparent to me when I arrived in Helsinki in the summer of 2000. The first image I saw when I turned on a television was of Toronto's Queen Street (home of MuchMusic) and the picture of a red Toronto streetcar, followed by shots of Montreal's downtown core. These familiar images were quite startling to me, particularly when I was in an environment so geographically distant from home. When I mentioned my surprise to Marco Bresba, he told me that this type of urban fluidity was, in fact, ideal: the ultimate objective of the station was to have feed from Helsinki, Barcelona, Toronto, and other urban centers that share one visual style so viewers won't necessarily know the city of origin.[21] This unified style is evidence of what Manuel Castells calls the new global urban "flows," whereby medium-sized cities become increasingly interconnected and the relations between individual cities and their outlying regions become secondary and less important.[22] Such was the impression conveyed by my informants: television had rendered Helsinki the most important geopolitical locale in Finland, followed by other international cities, larger Finnish cities, and finally, the outlying Finnish regions.

The effects of these urban-based Citytv environments extended beyond the loss of connection to outlying regions. These environments were so similar that they were undifferentiated. Like airport departure lounges, service stations, and high-speed trains, the *Jyrki*/MuchMusic set was one of the new ambiguous, global locales. Unlike an "anthropological place" that provides cultural identity and memory, binding its inhabitants to the history of the locale through the daily repetitions of "organic" social interactions, the *Jyrki*/MuchMusic environment, like the modern airport or supermarket, was a type of *nonplace* that was entirely interchangeable with other international MuchMusic sets. John Tomlinson describes nonplaces as bleak locales of contemporary modernity: places of solitude (even in the presence of others), silence, anonymity, alienation and impermanence. They are places where interaction is instrumental and "contractual". . .lifted out of any organic relation with a community existing in continuity through time.[23]

It is ironic that the MuchMusic set that first developed as an anthropological place on Queen Street, Toronto, was transformed through repetition to become a global nonplace. However, as John Tomlinson points out, it is important not to become too nostalgic about "anthropological places" for everything comes to some degree from somewhere else.[24] Nevertheless, there are differing degrees of foreign injection that alter whether we experience our environments as anthropological places or as nonplaces; the latter (including the ambiguous MuchMusic set) contribute to "mundane locational" experiences—in other words, supermodernity.[25]

As international urban flows displace urban-rural flows (as they do at *Jyrki*), these new supermodern relations have actual effects on viewers. One significant repercussion is a sense of cultural deterritorialization, a response often identified as a central condition of globalization. Nestor Garcia Canclini identifies deterritorialization as a separation of "natural" relations from social and geographical places.[26] Through the effects of globalization, these sites have become, in his words, "more ambiguous, 'decentred,' [and] 'placeless,'" to which people relate effortlessly, but without much sense of "local" cultural control.[27] The response to supermodernity, then, is less of alienation and more of ambivalence.

In his study of global effects on societies, Garcia Canclini interviewed residents in Tijuana, Mexico, and asked them to identify places and images in the city that they judged more representative of its particular life and culture. The responses, surprisingly, were the shops and tourist places, in other words, those places that lie beyond Tijuana. This, he argues, is a highly deterritorialized self-identity.[28] Following Garcia Canclini's model, I posed similar questions to my Finnish informants to ascertain their general sense of deterritorialization within their respective cities. The responses from the Turku and Helsinki informants differed considerably. I shall begin with the responses from Turku. When I asked, as part of a written questionnaire, what was "the most important features that a visitor to Turku might see when he or she visits here that distinguishes you as Finns or as residents of Turku," without exception they named historical and/or natural sites. In Turku there are many of these sites, including a medieval cathedral, the thirteenth-century Turku castle, and the River Aura that winds through the city. Respondents felt that Turku was distinguished by

(1) "The Cathedral and the Castle"
(2) "The river, Turku Castle."
(3) "The nature"
(4) "Nature: the river, the sea . . . and saunas by the lakes."
(5) "The river Aura."

Helsinki residents, however, had very different responses. Helsinki is located on a peninsula on the southern tip of Finland overlooking the Gulf of Finland and Europe's largest grouping of islands (a stunning 6,500-island archipelago). Streets curve around bays and parks and walkways edge a combination of neoclassical, art nouveau, National Romantic, and modern architecture. Despite an amazing harbor, two striking cathedrals (the white Lutheran Cathedral and Uspensky Cathedral, the largest Orthodox church in Scandinavia), *none* of the responses referred to these historical or to natural landmarks of the city. Responses included:

(1) "Helsinki does not differ so much from other European cities (Stockholm, Copenhagen, London). It's only smaller and less populated."
(2) "I think that nowadays Helsinki is a very modern, pleasant, and European city with a lot of possibilities."
(3) "We are not used to really big cities."

Some interpreted the question socially:

(1) "We're always a bit separated from others."
(2) "We're not particularly open or spontaneous."

Helsinki residents in particular seemed to lack a sense of connection to their landmarks, a sense their landmarks somehow belonged to them.

To ascertain whether Finnish viewers felt a sense of ownership or connection with *Jyrki,* I brought this definition of deterritorialization back to them and asked whether or not they considered *Jyrki* to be a domestic Finnish product. The responses were mixed from both the Turku and Helsinki residents. From Turku two informants explained:

(1) "In a way, yes, they are promoting Finnish bands and Finnish music, and in a way no, because they try to be so international."
(2) "Despite the Finnish hosts and bands the format is still rather foreign."

From Helsinki:

(1) "Yes, probably, but as I know the Canadian background to the show I would have to say no."
(2) "Somehow it is (because they speak Finnish maybe) but the form is from Canada."

This material then seems to present a paradox. When asked which places get the most focus on *Jyrki*, they all agreed it was Helsinki, but there the *Jyrki* environment is both a place (Helsinki) and increasingly also a non-place to which people feel an ambivalent connection. What then could make it "theirs"? Language? Artists? Location? As a globalized nonplace, could it ever be "theirs?"

I believe Citytv's presence in Finland had at least two repercussions. First, through stronger global city flows we witnessed the increasing loss of regional musics and a preference for the international repertoire (standardized in English). Second, the Citytv/*Jyrki* environment, with its interchangeable crews and locations, contributed to an increased sense of deterritorialization (not even the Finnish version of *Speakers Corner* had an *actual* corner), and an ambivalent sense of ownership and connection to place. This is, once again, perhaps the most ironic realization, given that Citytv prides itself on the power of local specificity.

In the end, neither *Jyrki* nor Moon TV were able to survive; both were dropped from the television listings in 2003. According to Marko Kulmala, these programs and stations likely did not survive because of financial difficulties experienced across Finnish media.[29] But MTV already has launched a series of new Scandinavian stations of which one is MTV Finland. From online discussion boards, viewers already are commenting on the extent to which MTV Finland resembles the earlier MTV Nordic. As one viewer writes:

Why should I watch?. . .It's going to have all the same programs *(The Osbournes, Jackass, South Park)*. . .and the music will mostly be American pop. The only difference will be that there will be Finnish subtitles (bad for my English) and the show hosts will be speaking Finnish . . . I watched MTV Finland . . . with my brother. Neither one of us was impressed."[30]

The viewer later lamented the loss of *Jyrki,* noting "Finnish bands haven't made many videos after *Jyrki* quit." Will this sentiment grow strong enough to provoke MTV Finland to imitate what *Jyrki* established more than a decade ago? Or does MTV's continued success indicate that there is no place for the local beyond the symbolic geography of Finland? If MuchMusic returns, will it attempt a regional focus and include the outlying Finnish areas or will it explore more city flows? It will be interesting to see how the stations respond to different pressures to create various types of imagined communities in future projects—pan-European, Scandinavian, Finnish, rural and urban locales—in order both to strengthen station-viewer identification and to share in the international music video marketplace of the twenty-first century.

CHAPTER SIX

Conclusion

*Far from being grounded in a mere "recovery" of the past, which is waiting to be
found, and which, when found, will secure our sense of ourselves into eternity,
identities are the names we give to the different ways we are positioned by, and
position ourselves within, the narratives of the past.*
—Stuart Hall, "Cultural Identity and Diaspora"

In my introduction I recounted the events of a conference in which the
complexity of divergent music video station narratives was elided in order
to foreground individual video content. This strategy, I argued, overlooked
the North American stations' rich divergences and, in turn, rendered invisible important cultural producers such as MuchMusic. In this concluding
chapter I explore some of the key similarities and differences between the
two stations both in their domestic and international markets and in what
we can learn more broadly about cultural power from analyzing just this
one facet of the popular media.

Some video parameters analyzed as part of this study point to the striking similarities between MTV and MuchMusic's video repertoires aired
that week. When I began this analysis I expected to find that some of the
video variables, when combined, would expose similarities, while others
would uncover differences on either side of the forty-ninth parallel. I sus-
pected that these differences, in turn, would contribute to what Hall might
describe as the two countries' distinct "narratives of the past." Of all of the
parameters analyzed for this research, describing and coding the videos'
lyric content took by far the most time and effort. This endeavor was
deemed worthwhile, however, because I anticipated that some differences
would emerge between the two stations owing to their divergent emphases
on musical genres, races, nationalities, or other equally important variables.

Through Web sites, liner notes, reviews, and careful repeated listening, I
coded the videos' lyrics. Yet, as the reader may have noticed, there was no
discussion of lyric content differences on MTV and MuchMusic because

there were no statistical differences between the two stations. When all of the messages and their combinations were analyzed by race, gender, and nationality, the two stations were consistently aligned. What I presumed could be a highly differentiated parameter, was, interestingly, the most closely related. With this observation my assumptions about how nation-bound narratives are constructed were shaken. This discovery was informative and limiting at the same time: it meant that one, if not the most telling, source of textual information was undifferentiated and unavailing. Unable to rely upon the lyrical texts for either direction or corroboration, I endeavored to seek out narratives in more covert places before realizing that the narratives embedded within the multitextual layers of MuchMusic and MTV are not necessarily self-evident (as I was hoping to find within lyric messages); instead, they are embedded within complex, sometimes seemingly contradictory sets of texts, from videos to trailers to VJs.

Because some of these nation-specific narratives have been reinforced for some time within both cultural policy and the popular media, they are now part of the consciousness of many viewers of the dominant hegemony (like myself) and therefore often go unnoticed. For this reason, it was important to undertake a content analysis of the musical and extramusical components and see how the resulting data all shone light on different angles of the predominant Canadian and American cultural narratives. For instance, my analysis of the extramusical content pointed to numerous programming differences between the two stations. MuchMusic made more content changes than MTV; taking into account time-zone differences, VJs who reflected a wider range of races and ethnicities, the presence of a diverse Toronto crowd, and a historically deeper range of videos that appealed to a wider age range, we see that the Canadian viewer was situated within a pluralistic community, both imaginary and real. MTV's community, meanwhile, was defined by the viewer's individuality: viewers' time zones were always respected, VJs engaged in direct address with the viewer, no crowd appeared on the station, and MTV's video repertoire targeted youth. Like CNN's *Headline News,* MTV emphasized a repetitious currency by means of a younger video repertoire (dating primarily from the years just prior to 1995) and an emphasis on alternative, rap, and urban musics, as opposed to the more traditional and older rock genres. In addition, MTV was not content to allow audiences just to listen to the programming. They interrupted household flow, bringing viewers back to the television set, whereas MuchMusic made it more possible for viewers to wander away. Through these techniques the stations revealed their disparate media biases in constructing space, time, and identity for viewers. The narrative of American hypercurrency and individuality versus Canadian plurality and orality were perpetuated within the extramusical content on both sides of the border. Since 1995, both stations have included more syndicated programming, and MTV has made some notable changes, including the addition of *TRL*, which is taped within the heart of Times Square. Despite this newer show, MTV today still lacks the geographical specificity and temporal specificity that MuchMusic consistently has injected into its style and programming.

In chapter 3, I explored the stations' video repertoires and examined another set of narratives that differentiated the two countries in 1995 and still continues to do today both within music video repertoires and the popular culture industries as a whole: the paucity of Canadian media personalities and the celebration of American celebrities. On MuchMusic, Canadian artists' star potential was diminished vis-à-vis the lack of live concert videos and artistic collaborations, whereas on both stations Americans enjoyed not only more live audiences but larger venues that served to heighten their status. Equally powerful was the Canadian narrative as the "kinder, gentler" nation relative to the United States. This "feminization" was linked with the Canadian acoustic female instrumentalists who played historically older instruments (and this ties into the narrative of the Canadian preference for time-bias, as established in the analysis of the extramusical content). These women stood in contrast to their American counterparts, the latter of whom were electrically defined as louder, more assertive, and able to occupy more sonic space.

I then explored the stations' racial representations in chapter 4. Whereas more African Americans in particular were featured in MTV's 1995 video repertoire than in its early years, evidence suggested that the "race problem" was far from "solved." While a considerable number of videos featuring black female performers had been added to the repertoire between 1981 and 1995, these women appeared in highly choreographed—and highly sexualized—dance far more often than any other demographic group (such was also true on MuchMusic). Since that date, this trend of hypersexualization has only become more pronounced as black women's bodies are even more blatantly objectified for male consumption.

We cannot be convinced that racism has been effectively challenged even though oppositional voices, in the first half of the 1990s, were considerably edged out with more palatable urban music and musicians replacing politicized rap. As Christopher John Farley has argued, the shift from rock and pop to rap and urban musics during the 1990s was substantial[1] and this trend clearly was reflected in MTV's playlist. In the early to mid-1980s MTV moved from a neglectful stance toward black artists—and particularly rap artists—to heralding not only their importance but their musical necessity. In 1995, volumes of "safer" rap and urban videos were aired on prime-time shows, gently displacing programs like the once cutting-edge *Yo! MTV Raps* to an overnight time slot (significantly, without a regular VJ, which contributed to its loss of viewer-VJ identification). These changes in repertoire, however, can also be interpreted as contributing to a pattern of American insularity (identified in the extramusical content from chapter 2). The vast majority of black artists were African American and few were from any other African diaspora. West Coast and East Coast rap and urban musics dominated, pushing out Jamaican reggae (*Reggae Sound System* was marginalized within the overnight time slot), reinforcing the myth that American artists were not only the best, but the only performers worth hearing.

MuchMusic's bi- and multiracial programming then was examined against the backdrop of Canadian multiculturalism. That this narrative would be evident within MuchMusic's fabric (multicultural representations of the African diaspora, more languages, and a wide range of nationalities), more so than within MTV's, is unsurprising. Indeed, in 1995, MuchMusic could be praised for its multicultural content including "world music" videos and the image of cultural plurality that was reinforced within the extramusical content. Multiculturalism was heightened further when combined with the racial and ethnic diversity of the VJs and time-of-day scheduling, both of which allowed viewers to be made aware of one another as they tuned in and out throughout the day.

Perhaps more important, however, were the ways in which these narratives/representations were nuanced on MuchMusic. Mainstream videos by established artists Janet Jackson or Bryan Adams represented multiculturalism with a familiar face. Meanwhile, other, more exotic musics/performers were held at the programming margins on half-hour shows like *Cliptrip* in the huge shadow cast by the significant white male rock/hard rock repertoire. (*Cliptrip* since has moved from MuchMusic to its sister station MuchMoreMusic, which, like VH1, targets an older demographic. *Going Coastal,* a program featuring music and musicians from Canada's outlying regions has since been added to the MuchMusic schedule, although this show does not reflect Canada's multicultural diversity to the same extent as *Cliptrip.*)

Examining the North American context revealed much information about the two stations; still, it remained critical to consider MuchMusic and MTV within one single market for a more rounded picture of how they have not only expanded, but adapted to international settings. *Jyrki* was used as a case study to show how even one after-school program could influence Finnish musical practices. Aspiring artists saw in *Jyrki* a unique opportunity, a stepping-stone to domestic and international success, something they could never imagine in MTV. But the effects did not stop there. Through *Jyrki* and Citytv's presence in Finland we witnessed a heightened loss of regional connection and an increased sense of global flows—and through their interchangeable crews and locations, we saw a more heightened sense of deterritorialization. Many viewers perceived *Jyrki* as an urban nonplace, contributing to their already developing sense of supermodernity. This ambivalent response is unlike how most Canadians would relate to MuchMusic, suggesting that that station's format did not adapt seamlessly to the Finnish context. Moreover, when *Jyrki* premiered it differentiated itself from MTV Nordic yet increasingly came to resemble the larger station—conflating, in the minds of Finnish viewers, Canadian and American cultural exports. So while many Canadians resent American cultural imperialism and take relief in knowing that they are protected from an influx of American cultural products by government policy, they may be surprised to know that within the Finnish context, their homegrown export was not easily distinguished from that of their American neighbor. The national narratives MuchMusic perpetuated within the Canadian context to ensure its own survival were only partially intelligible outside of the country's border.

The analysis of MuchMusic's and MTV's domestic stations in the first four chapters demonstrated that individual texts acquire meaning through one another; the case study of *Jyrki* further highlights that cultural texts are very context-dependent and constantly in fluctuation. This position challenges the work of some authors who prefer to read texts as explicit, self-contained, cultural articulations. In *The Presumption of Culture: Structure, Strategy, and Survival in the Canadian Cultural Landscape,* for instance, Tom Henighan makes a clear distinction between what clearly constitutes a "Canadian" artist or text from that which does not. From his perspective,

Canadian popular entertainers who "make it". . . need no support from government, and in most cases deserve none, because in the act of making it, they have shed most of what might constitute the uniqueness of their Canadian perspective. There are some entertainers for whom this is clearly not true, and who occupy the boundary between cultural levels, a Leonard Cohen, a Gordon Lightfoot, a Gilles Vigneault. This kind of artist clearly has a strong claim to be treated as a potent Canadian (or Québécois) cultural force, but this is clearly not true for music stars such as Bryan Adams or k. d. lang. . . . We should celebrate the achievements of our popular entertainers, just as we should applaud the foresight and finesse of such media entrepreneurs as Moses Znaimer and Michael MacMillan, the little-known but enterprising chairman of Atlantis Films. We can be grateful for whatever positive results such success stories create for Canada, but it is a mistake, I think, to lump these kinds of achievements together with those of our aesthetic culture. We are talking about entertainment here, and entertainment, if it is successful, pays.[2]

I have quoted Henighan at length here because I would like to challenge two of his assertions. First, he claims that the "Canadian perspective," evidenced in music by Cohen or Lightfoot, must be somehow tangible within the actual song either sonically, lyrically, or both. Of course, one could not disagree with the explicit "Canadianness" of, say, the lyrics in Lightfoot's "Canadian Railroad Trilogy." But I argue here, as I have done throughout this entire work, that such evidence is not always clearly visible or audible within one song. Instead, I suggest that every song is at once a single text as well as one piece of a much larger picture. It is for this reason that Bryan Adams's songs in isolation may apparently contribute little to a Canadian narrative; yet when Adams is read alongside Neil Young (as the only two Canadian artists to perform within medium-sized forums), or "Have You Ever Really Loved A Woman?" is read alongside Jackson's "Runaway" (as MuchMusic's most frequently aired choreographed videos from the sample), they make meanings *between* them and therefore *can* be read as contributors to larger, pervasive, Canadian narratives. Musical texts (videos, songs), then, should not necessarily be evaluated as "sufficiently" or "insufficiently" Canadian in isolation, as Henighan has done here, but read together to explore the sum of their effects. Even then, when consumed in another part of the world, this set of videos could easily be read as quintessentially "American."

Second, Henighan argues for the separation of "aesthetic" and "entertainment" culture within Canada (a tenuous distinction) and conveys his distaste for financially successful cultural articulations (read: popular). But what he does not seem to acknowledge is that boundaries between "artistic levels" have weakened, resulting in the melding of formerly exclusive forms/events: for example, short-length classical music videos, or The Three Tenors performing at the 1994 World Cup Soccer Championship Concert in Los Angeles, or Luciano Pavarotti's performance at the closing ceremonies of the 2006 Olympic Winter Games, just before Ricky Martin.[3] Henighan feels the need to preserve forms of "high" culture—although this is accomplished on a daily basis through private arts agencies, government funds, and the academy—but his distinctions between these two levels are somewhat arbitrary and inaccurate, particularly in light of the recent trends described above. And, as Rob Walser argues, the danger in forming this binary is that we risk positioning "high" culture beyond reproach and "low" culture as unworthy of our attention; both premises preclude critical acumen.[4] By imposing these artificial divisions, Henighan also misses the opportunity to see how parallel narratives articulated in seemingly unrelated ways actually work to reinforce the same image, *be* that national, racial, and/or gendered. I hope future studies will recognize the flow between these levels and not feel the need to impose such sharp distinctions between increasingly permeable categories.

In the introduction, I stated that my analysis would largely target Much-Music and that MTV would function as a comparative, secondary source. Such has largely been the case. The reason for this decision stemmed from the lack of scholarly and popular attention to MuchMusic, particularly in relation to the considerable interest in MTV. Now, however, it is possible to reflect upon one additional reason to pay attention to MuchMusic: this station offers domestic narratives that, within the North American context, are clearly distinctive from MTV's.

Indeed, during my interviews informants offered impassioned testimonies to MuchMusic's "un-American," unique, inclusive, open, diverse format, despite the fact that these musics do not yet draw a substantial enough audience to be financially beneficial to the station. Hearing these commentaries, I often felt uncomfortable with my pointed probing. Is it even possible for MuchMusic to respond to my criticisms and remain competitive? Is it possible for MuchMusic to stand up internationally against networks like MTV? Fortunately, over the course of my research, I realized that others shared my aspirations for MuchMusic and that there are many sound reasons for such critical questioning. As Avi Lewis put it,

Here's the reason that we judge MuchMusic more harshly: The possibilities are endless. The style encourages spontaneity and real youth voices and genuine youth experiences. MTV is such an impenetrable shining surface that . . . the possibility of that never occurs to you.[5]

I, too, appreciate MuchMusic's unique contribution to popular culture within Canada, its spontaneity, and its accessibility. Those possibilities, however, should not exempt the station from cultural criticism; in fact, these features should draw attention to the station as we continue to explore its unique potential as a developing cultural industry. The critical issue, as the VJ put it, goes beyond how MuchMusic has carved out a unique site within our cultural landscape to "whether [the station] makes use of it." How MuchMusic makes use of its abundant resources is a question that should be asked on an ongoing basis.

In 1994, Will Straw praised MuchMusic for its promotion of popular culture in Canada

not by casting a uniform national eye on our musical culture, but through constantly shifting perspectives which frustrate attempts to reduce that culture to a solitary essence. . . . [As a result] . . . [s]cholars who tune in briefly to MuchMusic, seeking a quick definition of Canadian music, find the answer to their question perpetually postponed.[6]

I agree. Rather than seek a "solitary essence," scholars might instead look to the relationships *between* musics, between hegemonic and marginalized genres and performers, and how these relationships might be context-dependent within the international marketplace. I have illustrated that it may be less useful to differentiate these two stations by means of excavating *a* "Canadian" or "American" music per se. Instead, MTV and MuchMusic can be differentiated by the ways in which they contribute to/corroborate/ frustrate existing narratives and establish new ones vis-à-vis complex relations of musical—and, by extension, social—power.

Appendixes

Variables Coded

Below I outline the specific variables coded as part of the current study. It is divided into two sections: The variables coded as part of the twelve-hour extramusical segment and those coded for the weeklong video sample. I begin with the shorter of the two sections, the twelve-hour extramusical analysis, for which twelve variables were coded.

The Twelve-hour Extramusical Analysis

1. *The station and tape number.* Twenty-eight six-hour tapes were used to record one week from each station, for a total of fifty-six tapes. For organizational purposes, each tape was provided a unique identification number.

2. *The date of the recording and time of day.* For the extramusical analysis, this parameter was coded at the level of the second in order to compare and contrast the length of nonmusical material, and to analyze commercial flow at the hourly level. When combined with tape number, it also aided in providing a unique marker for every televisual event.

3. *Program title.* This information was coded to facilitate an analysis of programming flow. In particular, I was interested in examining (a) the frequency with which programs changed during the day and at what times that occurred, and (b) differences in "dayparting" structures (that is, daily scheduling practices).

4. *Voice-over introduction.* As noted by Andrew Goodwin, one of the important functions VJs serve is to anchor the fast and rapidly changing visuals through their consistent, familiar image.[1] While most videos are indeed introduced by a visible VJ, I observed during my preliminary research that particular shows on both stations lack the visual referent, replaced instead with just the sound of the VJ during a station logo or dubbed over at the beginning of a video. I was interested in determining, then, the differing VJ functions according to how often the VJs were visually absent on each station, on which programs this occurred, and at what times of day.

5. *Name of VJ.* Documenting this parameter provided key information, including the number of VJs featured on each station, how many of these were guests and how many were "regulars," and to what extent more VJs "dilute" their function of "grounding" the stations.

6. *Appearance of guest VJs/artists.* The questions that prompted me to attend to this variable included: Do guest artists perform on the two stations? If so, how does this affect the studio dynamics and, subsequently, the viewers' relationship to the studio? If there is no apparent effect, what is the function of the guest artists or VJs? How do they relate with the "regular" VJ? The audience? The camera? These data were documented to better understand MuchMusic's and MTV's strategies of celebrity construction.

7. *Visual and sound trailers.* The purpose behind collecting these data was to examine the means by which the stations attempt to interrupt household flow. Do voices bring us back to the television more often on one station than another? How often are trailers linked with the familiar VJs' voices? How often are visuals and voices combined to reinforce the message and keep us tuned in?

This parameter was particularly difficult to code because of the number of possible combinations. For instance, some trailers are only visual; that is, words written at the end of a video identifying the video to follow after the commercial break and/or footage of the artist performing that would visually prompt the viewer to watch future events. Others included the sound of a voice, which may or may not be the VJ's, without a visual cue. Accordingly, I chose to make the first distinction between trailers that involved the VJs from those that did not. I then identified the type of event. For instance, was the event an upcoming video, concert clip, or other station event? Third, I considered the time of the advertised events: Were they immediate ("coming right up,") later in the hour, later the same day, that week, or that month? Finally, I chose to codify them according to whether or not they combined sound with a visual stimulus. This organizational process resulted in fifty-six different combinations for visual and sound trailers.

8. *Special video identification.* Although this parameter technically relates to the video repertoire examined in the next section and was therefore coded throughout the entire sample, I include it here because it relates closely to the extramusical material. By "special video identification" I refer to unique logos that appear at the beginning of the video and that sometimes remain in the corner throughout the video's entirety. The station's purpose of including this identification (for instance, "Classic Cut" or "OBG" for historically older videos), is to explain why it is appearing within a certain program. Further, it is added protection against losing the viewer to the household flow: If audience members do not like the video, they are assured that it will be over shortly and that another video more to their liking will be aired. The purpose of recording these data was to examine which videos were featured: Were they older or newer videos? How many debuts did they air? What are their repertoire biases? Did they promote a historical depth or new and innovative video styles?

9. *Nonstation commercials.* The reasons for documenting commercials are numerous. First, following Raymond Williams's previous work, I was interested in documenting both the number of commercial breaks per hour as well as the number of commercials that appeared during each break. Second, I documented the content for each commercial; that is, a general description of the commercial's narrative, and the name of the marketed product (and

spokesperson where applicable), as well as the style and tempo of the music. Following Kevin Williams's previously cited thesis, I then used this information to explore differences in commercial flow.

10. *Station commercials.* MTV and MuchMusic present an array of self-promoting station advertising. Some of these advertisements take the form of actual commercials (30–45 seconds in length) whereby a mood or attitude is established at the same time the station is advertised. How frequent are these commercials? What type of mood do they establish? Are they vehicles for the stations to align themselves with the viewing audience? Do they contribute to the construction of the viewers' imagined community?

   A second type of commercial is embedded in station contest advertisements. Much, for instance, was promoting a Def Leppard contest the week of the sample, while MTV featured the MTV Europe Video Awards. These contests were coded because they contribute tremendously to station mood and identity.

11. *Tags.* A second method of self-referential display appeared in the form of "tags." Two general types of tags were identified: those that featured the station logo (those advertising MTV and MuchMusic) and the program logo (*The Real World, Da Mix,* and so on). The purpose of tags is to provide a familiar image and help "anchor" the televisual flow.

    Station tags differ from commercials in several ways. While they do convey a mood, they are not ideologically weighted so heavily as are the station commercials. They also differ from commercials because they generally are shorter in length (5–15 seconds) and have less verbal text. They can feature either film footage or animation (as is frequently the case on MTV).

12. *Program logos.* The program logo functions to unify the images visually and to remind viewers of the program they are watching. It may be superimposed on a VJ or other image. Or it may also appear within the commercial segment of a program, most often in conjunction with the advertiser (*MuchMusic Countdown* with Guess Jeans, and the *MTV Jams Countdown* with Sega Games). The type and frequency of these program logos were documented.

    Program logos may appear within the top corner of video themselves. These logos were not accounted for here. The diminished size of the logo is evidence that it is secondary to the video itself; in addition to appearing with the title and artist credit over the video and so on, it sometimes is accompanied by the countdown number and other "distracting" features. Accordingly, these logos were not considered substantial enough to warrant documenting.

Finally, to account for every televisual event during this twelve-hour sample, I documented the lengths of the opening and closing credits, and well as "special breaks," the short station features that are not commercials per se but "community" segments, including, for instance, MuchMusic's "Word for Word" (promoting literacy). While the content of this material was not of particular importance, documenting them allowed me to account for every televised event.

In addition to these extramusical variables, the video coding involved a thorough description of the video repertoires over the entire week. After documenting the tape number, date, timing, and program title (for reasons already stated), twenty-two video-specific variables were coded.

The Weeklong Video Sample

1. *Video title.*

2. *Name of featured artist* and, where applicable, secondary featured artist. For instance, "Gangsta's Paradise" was performed by Coolio with a guest appearance by Notorious B.I.G. Accordingly, both artists were identified as contributors. With only few exceptions all artists were both heard and seen in their videos.

3. *Gender of performer.* Unlike Steven Williams's earlier cited binary coding procedure, I allowed three coding possibilities: male, female, and male + female. If a solo artist performed with unidentified backup musicians (for instance, Mitsou or Melissa Etheridge), and the other band members remained unnamed, the video was coded according to the gender of the featured artist.

4. *Race of performer.* In the introduction I attempted to problematize essentialist racial markers. Yet I am compelled to evoke them in my analysis as "white" and "black" skin color often delineated programming patterns—which, in turn, distinguish musics at the center of power from those at the margins. As I demonstrated there, those categories are not only used but reinforced in sometimes (deceptively) unproblematic ways that reinscribe relations of power. To these divisions, I added a category of "white + black" for two reasons: (a) to determine the frequency with which whites appear overall and (b) to explore whether white artists function as "access points" for nonwhite musicians.

   Finally, groups were identified individually (First Nations, Hispanic, and so on), based on particular pieces of information, including artist self-identification, musical genre, and language. They were then grouped into the "nonblack visible minority" category. The numbers of this grouping were often small, so much so that they were statistically insignificant. As a group, however, these individual videos pointed to possible modes of marginalization.

   I gave significant attention to locating the artists' racial/ethnic self-definition. To this end, magazines, newspapers, and Web sites were extremely helpful. Official and unofficial Web sites were consulted and artists' self-definitions were always sought. Usually, unofficial sites contained the most useful information; artists' racial identifications are occasionally changed by recording companies in the "official" pages according to shifts in marketing strategies.

5. *Nationality of performer.* Most artists' original nationalities (as determined by birthplace) were attainable through the Internet. Several nationalistic labels are possible here: artists sometimes change countries and citizenship. Of course, others do not. Take, for instance, Alanis Morissette. Although she resides for most of the year in the United States, she has maintained her Canadian citizenship. Accordingly, she is identified here as "Canadian." If the artist adopts a new citizenship, dual nationalities were noted (for instance, "Jamaican-Canadian"). When an artist moved among more than two countries, the term "multiple" is used (this category includes Heather Nova who lived on a sailboat until she was fifteen, then called Bermuda, the United States, and then England, "home").

   Of course, within a practical schema, MTV and MuchMusic viewers may receive artists entirely differently. Generally, Canadian artists tend to be identified more explicitly as such by Canadian media. Such is less the case within the

United States, where artists often are assumed to be American until they are identified otherwise. Accordingly, I recognize that the categories I have created here may not reflect the understanding of MTV's and MuchMusic's viewing audiences.[2]

6. *Performing force.* Steven Williams used performing force to help identify musical genre. Here it is treated both as an indicator of genre but also as a separate entity to differentiate artists *within* genres. In particular, the primary issue surrounding performing force was to identify the differences between male and female performing forces. Is there a difference between male and female performance within the same genres across the two stations? Do women sing with the same frequency on the two stations? Play instruments? Documenting the performing force involved differentiating among solo artists, duos, or groups. These combinations then were identified as singing, singing and playing instruments, or not shown performing. Finally, I noted when group members were featured and when background performers were included.

7. *Presence of instruments.* Like performing force, the presence of instruments differs between genres. Heavy metal bands tend to display their instruments, while pop or dance artists do so less frequently. But what is the relationship between gender and the display of instruments? Were female urban artists shown performing instruments or shown with other instrumentalists as frequently as male urban artists? For this variable, I identified when a video had no visible sound source, a limited visible sound source, or a fully visible source. Because the instrumental performing force of most genres is fairly standardized, I did not identify every instrument performed within each video. Instead, I identified unusual instrumental additions and/or omissions.

8. *Solos.* I predicted that my analysis of this variable would confirm established musical patterns; for example, that rock and metal videos feature more guitar solos than pop videos. To gather more useful information, this variable was coded alongside gender. How often did the female artists perform their own solos? When were nonfeatured artists brought in to solo? On what types of instruments did women and men solo? Did these results differ between the two stations? To answer these questions, I noted the featured solo instrument and whether the featured artist or a nonfeatured artist performed the actual solo.

9. *Musical genre.* Refer to my criteria for musical genres outlined in the introduction.

10. *Tempo.* Tempo was included for gauging differences between genres across the two stations. Tempi were coded according to their beats per minute. Because two tempi were evidenced in a number of songs, this category was divided into "Tempo 1" and "Tempo 2."

11. *Language of lyrics.* Steven Williams noted having little trouble identifying lyrics in his sample, and that the only three languages heard were English, French, Spanish and a combination thereof. The 1995 sample proved to be more difficult: all of those languages appeared plus, for instance, Punjabi and Ukrainian. An "undetermined" label was given to those few videos that were linguistically unclear.[3]

12. *Quantity of lyrics.* Musical genres can be identified not only by the sonorities of the music, but also the amount of text. Moreover, other important differentiating information can be drawn within genres from the amount of text. Does the amount of text correlate with gender and/or race of the performer? Which groups tend to mix textual levels? Are videos aired with no text on either station? What might be the significance of these videos, if any? The quantity of lyrics was coded accordingly as heavy (for example, rap music), medium (for example, most rock and pop musics), low (usually with text in only one section of song, as in El Patio's "Nacho Cano"), medium + heavy (featuring a middle-ground text and a heavily texted solo such as in the Blues Travelers' "Hook" or Mariah Carey's "Fantasy"), no lyric content, or a combination of these.

13. *Film color.* Expanding upon Steven Williams's categories, I chose to code this variable according to the following possibilities: color, black-and-white, monochrome (a single tint), affected color (saturated and technologically enhanced colors), and all possible combinations of these. Here, I was interested in exploring a number of questions: Did particular artists employ black-and-white techniques even when they were not financially restricted? Did the use of black-and-white or monochrome differ between the two stations?

14. *Additional visual/sonic features.* These features include the use of granular film, altered film, special lighting effects, blurred filming, diegetic silence, nondiegetic silence, diegetic music, and nondiegetic music. Each of these is defined as follows:

    (a) **Grain of film.** A granular filmic image can convey a sense of "realness" and authenticity to the viewer, thus altering an artist's persona. Did the use of grainy film differ among genres? Nationalities?

    (b) **Altered image.** Altering includes the use of techniques such as camera distortions or negative imaging. Altered filming would work opposite to granular filming, conveying a more specialized, high-technological interface between the viewer and performer.

    (c) **Special lighting effects.** These effects may include "flash" photography, overexposed lighting, or any other special effect. Usually these function in making the artist more "glamorous" and thus more distant from the viewing audience.

    (d) **Blurred filming.** This parameter can function in several ways, depending upon with which feature it is coupled. For instance, grainy, blurred, black-and-white images can give a "pseudodocumentary" feel to the video, thus making it more accessible. When coupled with altered film and saturated colors, however, the blurriness can make the video seem more distant, providing a buffer between viewer and artist.

    (e) **Diegetic silence.** For this parameter, I analyze "diegetic silence" (environmental sounds, such as birds, or voices in the absence of music), which, I argue, makes the video and artist seem more accessible and immediate. Who used it within the present sample?

    (f) **Nondiegetic silence.** This coding indicates that a video includes a passage (usually no more than a few seconds) that is entirely without sound. Nondiegetic silence is significant because it disrupts the flow of sounds from the television, thus attracting the viewers' attention and rupturing household flow. Did one station air more videos with nondiegetic silence? To what ends?

(g) **Diegetic music.** Also called "source music," the music heard seems to originate from within the imagery. It could include a radio, or the image of a band. Like diegetic silence, it makes the band seem contextualized and more familiar.

(h) **Nondiegetic music.** A video is labeled "nondiegetic" if there is speech in the imagery that temporarily takes precedence over the music. Reducing the music's volume and overlaying the spoken text on top usually accomplishes nondiegesis. In Def Leppard's "When Love and Hate Collide," for instance, the band performs separately from the imagery. The musical volume frequently is lowered so that the dialogue from the imagery can be temporarily foregrounded.

15. *Choreography.* In chapter 4 I argued that within the MTV Top 100 Videos choreography differed according to race and gender. For that analysis, I made distinctions among choreography, organized movement, and gesture. Those labels are repeated here for consistency.

16. *Musical performance axis.* Steven Williams's category of performance axis did not indicate the presence of an audience on camera, nor the relationship between the performative and imaginal levels. This recognition is important when examining the emotional connection between the performer and the video content. Taking these potential shortcomings into account, my musical performance axis was graded as follows:

Musical performance 0 (no performance);

Musical performance 1: onstage "live" musical performance(s) with audience/participants;

Musical performance 2: onstage "live" musical performance(s) without audience/participants;

Musical performance 3: nonimaginal setting musical performance without audience/participants;

Musical performance 4: nonimaginal setting musical performance(s) with audience/participants ;

Musical performance 5: imaginal setting musical performance(s) without audience/participants;

Musical performance 6: imaginal setting musical performance(s) with audience/participants;

Musical performance 7: imaginal-related musical performance(s) without audience/participants;

Musical performance 8: imaginal-related musical performance(s) with audience/participants.

"Nonimaginal" indicates that the artist's musical performance context is in no way related to the imagery (the band plays in a field and the imagery is set in a school). "Imaginal" suggests that the artists perform within the imaginal context (the imagery and musical performance take place within the same schoolrooms) whereas "imaginal-related" indicates that there is a resemblance between the two contexts but they are not identical (the musical performance and imagery both appear to be set in the same school but their exact locations are not identical).

17. *Musical performance contextualization.* As a complement to the eight musical performance axes, I chose to describe the musical performance context separately. This decision was based on my preliminary observations that women who perform pop music were more often presented within decontextualized settings than hard rock and metal performers, who appeared more in live concert venues. In my study of preadolescent video audiences, male hard rock and metal artists accordingly were interpreted as being more "real" than the female artists.[4]

The ramifications of these manufactured settings are serious. As noted previously, John Shepherd argues that people who are decontextualized from social relations bestow upon them additional power.[5] How then are performers from the present sample contextualized? Is the sample divided by gender and/or genre? Furthermore, do the artists appear in scenery that depicts a specific place (flying above the New York City or Toronto skyline), a familiar place (a street), an unfamiliar space (no clear background), or a completely imaginal setting (floating in the stars)? Or do they appear by means of displacement/special camera effects? Does this result in some artists being perceived as more "real" than others? To address these questions, the above-cited five degrees of contextualization are identified in the musical performance text for each video.

18. *Imagery axis.* Following Steven Williams, the following imaginal axes were coded for the present study:

Imagery 0 (no nonmusical performance images): only the performers are shown, either in concert, or in dance, but without an imaginal component;

Imagery 1 (musical performance–related imagery): almost a musical performance video in which only the artists are seen. They may be shown lip-syncing or with additional props, which adds another subtext (for instance, Lisa Loeb's previously cited video "Do You Sleep");

Imagery 2 (concert-related imagery): concert musical performance images, possibly more than one concert, or with audience images, or "en route" imagery;

Imagery 3 (narrative): images that tell a story, that reach some sort of conclusion or resolution to a problem or conflict;

Imagery 4 (pseudonarrative): images that suggest a temporal/narrative structure but defy rules of narrative structure. The viewer is required to fill in the "missing pieces" using his or her own imagination (Steven Williams's Imagery 2);

Imagery 5 (collage and pastiche): video images that lack a visual narrative thread altogether (Steven Williams's Imagery 5 and 6). Examples include the Foo Fighters' "I'll Stick Around" or Silverchair's "Tomorrow";

Imagery 6 (film images): the use of scenes from a particular film to complement the soundtrack (Steven Williams's Imagery 7).

19. *Imagery contextualization.* The imagery, like the musical performance component, is coded according to a familiar place, an unfamiliar space, a completely imaginal setting, or by means of displacement/special camera effects.

20. *Message.* Again, adapting Steven Williams's categories, the following messages were coded:

Message 1 (social relevance at the individual level): videos that make personal statements both visually and lyrically, which includes love songs;

Message 2 (conservative): socially conservative, or patriarchal/sexist messages that may or may not be connected to nostalgic reminiscences;

Message 3 (acceptable social commentary): videos that, while somewhat controversial, purport notions that are currently in the process of mainstream entrenchment, including AIDS awareness, opposition to inner city problems of drug abuse and gang violence;

Message 4 (oppositional social commentary): videos that challenge mainstream societal notions and argue for controversial social change. Topics include feminism/resistance to patriarchy, resistance to white supremacy, etc.;

Message 5 (irreverent): videos that are intentionally antisocial and implicitly socially critical;

Message 6 (postmodern): videos that are consciously antinarrative and refuse to provide any direction.

The only significant change to Steven Williams's categories is the name change of message 2 from "traditional and nostalgic" to "conservative."

21. *Artist performing in imagery.* Imaginal involvement is coded for the current study according to whether the artists act, perform, act + perform, or appear on video within the imaginal component.

22. *Video description.* A paragraph-length description was written for every video. Keywords were included for retrieval purposes.

APPENDIX B

Music Videos and Globalization Questionnaire

1. Background information:
   Gender: F   M
   Age: _____

2. In which language are you most comfortable speaking? _____

3. How many hours do you watch television per week? (Please circle)
   (a) less than 1 hour per week
   (b) 1–3
   (c) 4–7
   (d) 8–10
   (e) 11–13
   (f) 14–16
   (g) more than 17 hours per week

4. Could you please identify the programs that you watch most often and their stations?

   (a) _____ station: _____

   (b) _____ station: _____

   (c) _____ station: _____

   (d) _____ station: _____

5. Which music video stations or programs do you have available to you at home or with friends? Please list as many as you know:

   (a) _____

   (b) _____

   (c) _____

   (d) _____

6. Do you watch *Jyrki* on MTV3?   Yes ___ No ___

7. How often do you watch *Jyrki*?
   (a) Never
   (b) Once a month
   (c) Once a week, if I happen to be watching television anyway
   (d) Two to three times a week
   (e) Usually everyday

8. Do you watch MTV Nordic?   Yes ___   No ___

9. How often do you watch MTV Nordic?
   (a) Never
   (b) Once a month
   (c) Once a week, if I happen to be watching television anyway
   (d) Two to three times a week
   (e) Usually every day

10. Do you watch any MTV Nordic shows in particular? If so, please identify these shows:

    (a) _____

    (b) _____

    (c) _____

    (d) _____

11. Have you ever seen music videos on Moon TV?   Yes ___   No ___

12. How often do you watch Moon TV?
    (a) Never
    (b) Once a month
    (c) Once a week, if I happen to be watching television anyway
    (d) Two to three times a week
    (e) Usually everyday

13. Do you like any Moon TV shows in particular? Please identify these shows:

    (a) _____

    (b) _____

    (c) _____

    (d) _____

14. Do you watch any other music videos stations or programs? If so, which ones do you watch?

   (a) _____

   (b) _____

   (c) _____

   (d) _____

15. If someone just arrived in Finland and asked you the differences between *Jyrki*, MTV Nordic, and any other video source, what would you say?

   _____

   _____

   _____

   _____

16. Can you identify one thing you do and don't like about:
   Jyrki?

   I Like: _____

   I Dislike: _____

   MTV Nordic?

   I Like: _____

   I Dislike: _____

   Moon TV?

   I Like: _____

   I Dislike: _____

   Another source?

   I Like: _____

   I Dislike: _____

17. Do you believe these music programs/stations have contributed to shaping music in Finland? If so, how?

   _____

   _____

   _____

   _____

18. What genres of music do you listen to most? Please number them from your most preferred (1) to your least preferred:

___ rock
___ alternative
___ rhythm and blues
___ pop
___ hiphop
___ industrial
___ dance
___ metal
___ other: _____.
___ other: _____.
___ other: _____.

19. Which Finnish soloists/bands are your favorites?

(a) _____

(b) _____

(c) _____

20. Which non-Finnish soloists/bands are your favorites?

(a) _____

(b) _____

(c) _____

21. Is it important to you that Finnish artists sing in Finnish or Swedish? Why or why not?

_____

_____

_____

_____

22. What do you believe are the most important features that a visitor to Turku might see when she visits here that distinguishes you as Finns or as residents of Turku?

_____

_____

_____

_____

23. Which television programs would you encourage a visitor to watch to understand your experience as a Finn? Why?

_____

_____

_____

_____

24. Do you feel that you are part of a "Nordic" community? Why or why not?

_____

_____

_____

_____

25. Do you think MTV Nordic is successful in creating a sense of "Nordicity" or "Europeanness"? Please explain.

_____

_____

_____

_____

26. Do you feel an increasing sense of being more international, European, Finnish, local, or all of these? Can you explain how?

_____

_____

_____

_____

27. *Jyrki* began several years after MTV was already established to serve a local viewing population. Do you feel that *Jyrki* successfully creates a local program that speaks to you personally? Why or why not?

_____

_____

_____

_____

28. Do you have an impression from your viewing experience of *Jyrki* regarding which places in Finland are given the most airtime? The least?

_____

_____

_____

_____

29. Do you consider *Jyrki* to be a domestic Finnish program?

_____

_____

_____

_____

30. Are you aware of any links between *Jyrki* and particular non-Finnish cities in the musical or extramusical content (from interviews, features, and so on)? Please explain.

_____

_____

_____

_____

31. *Jyrki* sometimes includes interviews from MuchMusic, the Canadian music video channel. Have you ever been aware of this connection? If so, has this shaped your perceptions of Canada or Canadians? Please explain.

_____

_____

_____

_____

32. This final question will be asked after viewing a short excerpt on tape.

_____

_____

_____

_____

If, after the workshop, you have any other comments, please feel free to write them below:

_____

_____

_____

_____

_____

_____

Notes

❦

Preface and Acknowledgments (pp. vii–viii)

1. See, for instance, E. Ann Kaplan, *Rocking Around the Clock: Music Television, Postmodernism, and Consumer Culture* (New York: Methuen, 1987), viii; and Jack Banks, "The Historical Development of the Video Music Industry: A Political Economic Analysis" (Ph.D. diss., University of Oregon, 1991), 28.

2. Tom Shales, "The Pop Network That's Dim and Ditzy to Decor," *Washington Post,* August 1, 1985, B9.

1. Introduction (pp. 1–22)

1. MTV (music television) began as a single American cable television channel in 1981; it now has stations worldwide (MTV Europe, MTV Asia, MTV Australia, and so forth). "MTV" here stands for MTV United States unless otherwise stated.

2. Historically, the MTV repertoire has been at the center of American video scholarship to the extent that often it is the understood source even if it is not explicitly identified in the article or book title. See, for instance, E. Ann Kaplan, *Rocking Around the Clock,* or Marsha Kinder, "Music Video and the Spectator: Television, Ideology, and Dream," in *Television: The Critical View,* 4th ed., ed. Horace Newcomb (London: Oxford University Press, 1987), 229–254, both of which examine only the MTV repertoire.

3. CHUM is a media company that owns several television systems and many Canadian radio stations.

4. For more on this criticism, see "Fuse TV" at http://www.reference.com/browse/wiki/Fuse_TV (accessed November 7, 2005).

5. Benedict Anderson, *Imagined Communities: Reflections on the Origin and Spread of Nationalism* (London: Verso, 1983).

6. These, of course, are long-standing narratives on either side of the border: as Eva Mackey argues, the quintessential American icon is of the cowboy, the "rugged individual," whereas the Canadian icon is the Mountie who represents the kind and gentle state—in other words, a Canadian collective. See Eva Mackey, *The House of Difference: Cultural Politics and National Identity in Canada* (Toronto: University of Toronto Press, 2002), 2.

7. Communications researcher Ira Wagman suspects that this paucity reflects the difficulty in conducting research on the Canadian music industry in general. See

Ira Wagman, "Rock the Nation: MuchMusic, Cultural Policy and the Development of English-Canadian Music-Video Programming, 1979–1984," *Canadian Journal of Communication* 26, no. 4 (2001): 2.

8. Jim Bessman, "MuchMusic is Much Different," *Billboard* (March 9, 1991): 63.

9. Jack Banks, *"Monopoly Television: MTV's Quest to Control the Music"* (Boulder, Colo.: Westview Press, 1996), 110.

10. Rich Brown, "Tom Freston: The Pied Piper of Television," *Broadcasting and Cable* (September 19, 1994): 37.

11. The minimum Canadian content regulation stipulates that a certain number of Canadian videos must be aired per hour. This is determined by the "MAPL" system whereby two of the following must be true: the music (M) is written exclusively by a Canadian; the artist (A) who performs the music or lyrics is a Canadian; the production (P) is such that the music is recorded or performed entirely in Canada; and the lyrics (L) are written exclusively by a Canadian.

For more information on Canadian content regulations see the Fraser Institute, "Definition of a Canadian Television Program," http://oldfraser.lexi.net/publications /forum/1998/august/canadian.html (accessed March 7, 2005).

12. Elspeth Probyn, *Outside Belongings* (New York: Routledge, 1996), 22.

13. Ernest Renan, "What is a Nation?" in *Nation and Narration*, ed. Homi Bhabha (New York: Routledge, 1990), 19–20.

14. Ien Ang, "Culture and Communication: Towards an Ethnographic Critique of Media Consumption in the Transnational Media System," *European Journal of Communication* 5 (1990): 239–240.

15. Richard Collins, *Television: Policy and Culture* (London: Unwin Hyman, 1990), 199.

16. Carole Carpenter, "The Ethnicity Factor in Anglo-Canadian Folklorists," in *Canadian Music: Issues of Hegemony and Identity,* ed. Beverley Diamond and Robert Witmer (Toronto: Canadian Scholars' Press, 1994), 131.

17. Mackey, *The House of Difference,* 2.

18. Richard Day, "Constructing the Official Canadian: A Genealogy of the Mosaic Metaphor in State Policy Discourse," *Topia* 2 (1998): 42–43.

19. Renan, "What is a Nation?" 11.

20. Stuart Hall, "Cultural Identity and Diaspora," in *Identity, Community, Culture, Difference,* ed. Jonathan Rutherford (London: Lawrence Wishart, 1990), 210.

21. Tamar Mayer, "Gender Ironies of Nationalism: Setting the Stage," in *Gender Ironies of Nationalism: Sexing the Nation,* ed. Tamar Mayer (New York: Routledge, 2000), 5.

22. Judith Butler, *Gender Trouble: Feminism and the Subversion of Identity* (New York: Routledge, 1990), 22.

23. Leslie K. Dwyer, "Spectacular Society: Nationalism, Development and the Politics of Family Planning in Indonesia," in *Gender Ironies of Nationalism: Sexing the Nation,* ed. Tamar Mayer (New York: Routledge, 2000), 26–27.

24. Jo-Anne Lee and John Lutz, "Introduction: Toward a Critical Literacy of Racisms, anti-Racisms, and Racialization," in *Situating "Race" and Racisms in Space, Time and Theory: Critical Essays for Activists and Scholars,* ed. Jo-Anne Lee and John Lutz (Montreal and Kingston: McGill-Queen's University Press, 2005), 14.

25. Ibid.

26. Stuart Hall, "The Question of Cultural Identity," in *Modernity: An Introduction to Modern Societies,* ed. Stuart Hall, David Held, Don Hubert, and Kenneth Thompson (Cambridge: Open University Press, 1996), 617.

27. Ibid.

28. Russell A. Potter, *Spectacular Vernaculars: Hip-Hop and the Politics of Postmodernism* (Albany: State University of New York Press, 1995), 136.

29. William Sonnega, "Morphing Borders: The Remanence of MTV," *Drama Review*, 39, no. 1 (1995): 50.

30. Frith, *Sound Effects: Youth, Leisure and the Politics of Rock 'n' Roll* (London: Constable, 1983), 13.

31. Roy Shuker, *Understanding Popular Music*, 2nd ed. (New York: Routledge, 2001), 150–151.

32. This strategy was modeled on Raymond Williams's *Television: Technology and Cultural Form* (New York: Schocken Books, 1974).

33. During the taping of the sample, approximately two hours of MTV videotape was mistakenly erased; the programs affected were *Rude Awakening* and *MTV Jams* on Tuesday morning, November 7. This accounts for approximately twenty additional videos.

34. An "event" is a self-contained unit such as a commercial or video. I shall occasionally make reference to "video events"; these indicate the total number of videos aired that share a particular feature, and that usually include repeated videos. For instance, fifty video events might include only five different videos repeated ten times each.

35. Kevin Williams, "Musical Visuality: A Phenomenological Essay on Music Television," (Ph.D. diss., Ohio University, 1995), 188.

36. Karen Pegley, "'Much' Media: Towards an Understanding of the Impact of Music Videos on Canadian Pre-Adolescent Identities," *Canadian Folk Music Journal* 20 (1992): 33–39.

37. Callum, Fagan, Hickey, Kellog, Martinez, Schindler, and Schwartz. "TV Guide Presents 40 Years of the Best," *TV Guide* (April 1993): 92.

38. Quoted in Shawn McCarthy, "Do we want cultural protection?" *Toronto Star*, February 1, 1997, F4.

39. For more figures on the American cultural presence in Canada, see McCarthy, "Do we want cultural protection?"; Marci McDonald, "A blow to magazines," *Macleans*, January 27, 1997, 58–59; and Sid Adilman, "Yikes! They're tipping the cultural balance," *Toronto Star*, January 26, 1997, B1, B8.

40. Richard Collins, *Culture, Communication, and National Identity: The Case of Canadian Television* (Toronto: University of Toronto Press, 1990), 108.

41. Robert Weber, *Basic Content Analysis* (Beverly Hills: Sage Publications, 1985), 9.

42. Brian Winston, "On Counting the Wrong Things," in *The Media Reader*, ed. Manuel Alvarado and John O. Thompson (London: British Film Institute, 1990), 62.

43. Ibid., 61.

44. Dominic Strinati, *An Introduction to Theories of Popular Culture* (New York: Routledge, 1995), 195.

45. Ibid., 193.

46. Ibid., 195.

47. Steven Williams, "An Analysis of Social Critique in Music Videos Broadcast on MuchMusic" (master's thesis, University of Alberta, 1993).

48. The former is the case in several theses including Kevin Williams' Ph.D. dissertation "Musical Visuality: A Phenomenological Essay on Music Television," in which specialty shows were taped over the course of a week, and videos over several months; or Kerry Carnahan's comparison of news on MTV (United States) and MTV Europe, for which she examined eight news programs on each station for a total of sixteen broadcasts aired during two 2-month periods (Kerry Carnahan, "Can Television Support an International Media Community? A Comparative Frame Analysis of MTV News In the United States and Europe" (master's thesis, University of Washington, 1994.) Block samples include Steven Williams's thesis on MuchMusic for which he examined a one-week sample.

49. Michel Foucault, *The Archaeology of Knowledge* (New York: Pantheon, 1972), 27–28.

50. MIT Communications Forum, "Changing Media, Changing Audiences," http://web.mit.edu/comm-forum/forums/changing_audiences.html (accessed September 29, 2006).

51. Ibid.

52. "Open (minds, finds, conversations)," http://open.typepad.com/open/2006 /07/0_60_in_under_1.html (accessed January 3, 2007).

53. In most scholarly considerations of music television, MuchMusic is usually relegated to a brief mention, as in *Sound and Vision: The Music Video Reader,* ed. Simon Frith, Andrew Goodwin, and Lawrence Grossberg (New York: Routledge, 1993); or, at most, a few paragraphs, such as in Banks's *Monopoly Television.* Scholarly literature on MuchMusic itself is highly limited; it includes the previously mentioned master's thesis by Steven Williams and work by Will Straw. MuchMusic circulates to researchers one particular article by Straw entitled "'Much' to Celebrate," a twelve-page document written for Much on the occasion of their tenth anniversary (1994).

54. David Morley and Kevin Robins, *Spaces of Identity: Global Media, Electronic Landscapes and Cultural Boundaries* (New York: Routledge, 1995), 45.

55. Philip Schlesinger, "On National Identity: Some Conceptions and Misconceptions Criticized," *Social Science Information* 26, no. 2 (1987): 235.

56. Harold Innis, *The Bias of Communication* (Toronto: University of Toronto Press, 1951) and Jody Berland, "Space at the Margins: Colonial Spatiality and Critical Theory After Innis," *Topia* 1 (1997): 65–66.

57. Because of the substantial size of the database, seemingly infinite combinatorial possibilities have arisen and are reportable. As a result, only those findings that appear to be significant for particular demographic groups are examined. Some of the data will be referenced in various chapters as they tie into another web of identity construction (for instance, musical genres).

58. Ang, "Culture and Communication," 245.

2. *"It's All Just Fluffy White Clouds" (pp. 23–44)*

1. These exceptions include Andrew Goodwin, *Dancing in the Distraction Factory: Music Television and Popular Culture* (Minneapolis: University of Minnesota Press, 1992), and Williams, "Musical Visuality."

2. Rick Altman, "Television/Sound," in *Studies in Entertainment: Critical Approaches to Mass Culture,* ed. T. Modleski (Bloomington: Indiana University Press, 1986), 43.

3. Ien Ang, *Living Room Wars: Rethinking Media Audiences for a Postmodern World* (London: Routledge, 1996), 145.

4. Williams, *Television: Technology and Cultural Form,* 99.

5. The videos originally were divided into twelve categories (the five primary categories of rock, alternative, pop, rap, urban, and a smaller number of videos that did not fit into these categories including industrial, folk/traditional, dance, and so on). Graphing this level of detail, however, did not provide statistically significant results for the smaller genres. Accordingly, the smaller categories were collapsed into one grouping entitled "other."

6. Williams, *Television: Technology and Cultural Form,* 93.

7. Altman, "Television/Sound," 42 (emphasis in original). I would argue that sound (music) without a verbal text allows the viewer to return to household flow, whereas music with a verbal text draws them back into the television flow. Ironically, nondiegetic silence (a portion of a video with no sound whatsoever) also draws the

viewer back to the television set: silence is very disruptive, and prompts many viewers to explore what is "wrong."

8. Joseph Boggs, *The Art of Watching Films*, 3rd ed. (Toronto: Addison-Wesley, 1991), 234.

9. Kurt Danziger, *Interpersonal Communication* (New York: Pergamon, 1976), 66.

10. Goodwin, *Dancing in the Distraction Factory*, 141–142.

11. Altman, "Television/Sound," 40–41.

12. Goodwin, *Dancing in the Distraction Factory*, 140.

13. John Langer, "Television's Personality System," *Media, Culture and Society* 4 (1981): 355.

14. Ibid., 352.

15. Ibid., 351.

16. Ibid., 357.

17. Ibid., 355.

18. Ibid., 363.

19. Erving Goffman, *The Presentation of Self in Everyday Life.* (Garden City, N.Y.: Doubleday, 1959), 22–30.

20. Joshua Meyerowitz, *No Sense of Place: The Impact of Electronic Media on Social Behavior* (New York: Oxford University Press, 1985), 64–66.

21. Ibid., 65.

22. John Shepherd, "Music and Male Hegemony," in *Music and Society: The Politics of Composition, Performance and Reception,* ed. Richard Leppert and Susan McClary (Cambridge: Cambridge University Press, 1987), 154.

23. The performances are in fact live, usually in front of an audience.

24. P. David Marshall, *Celebrity and Power: Fame in Contemporary Culture* (Minneapolis: University of Minnesota Press, 1997), 125.

25. Cited in Langer, "Television's Personality System," 354.

26. The videos included here are those that had a "request" logo shown at some point before or during the video.

27. Banks, *Monopoly Television*, 127.

28. David Tobenkin, "The all-music channels," *Broadcasting and Cable* 2 (September 1996): 38.

29. I thank Jody Berland for suggesting Innis's work.

30. Kim Sawchuck, "An Index of Power: Innis, Aesthetics, and Technology," in *Harold Innis in the New Century: Reflections and Refractions,* ed. C. Acland and W. Buxton (Montreal and Kingston: McGill-Queens University Press, 1999), 371.

31. Innis, *Bias of Communication*, 76.

32. As noted in the first chapter, MTV has since become more geographically situated through programs like *TRL,* responding to viewers' desire for more local inflections.

33. Jody Berland, "Space at the Margins: Colonial Spatiality and Critical Theory After Innis," *Topia* 1 (1997): 65–66.

34. Innis, *Bias of Communication*, 372.

3. "Simple Economics" (pp. 45–69)

1. For more on women's exclusion from public popular music performance practices, see, for instance, Sara Cohen, "Men Making a Scene: Rock Music and the Production of Gender," and Mavis Bayton, "Women and the Electric Guitar," both in *Sexing the Groove: Popular Music and Gender,* ed. Sheila Whiteley (New York: Routledge, 1997), 17–33 and 39–44, respectively.

2. "Live" here means the impression of performing live.

3. Jody Berland, "Sound, Image and Social Space: Music Video and Media Reconstruction," in *Sound and Vision: The Music Video Reader*, 39.

4. To view this video, go to http://www.youtube.com/watch?v=OjOPUe4 YKSU (accessed December 4, 2006).

5. See Carol Vernallis, *Experiencing Music Video: Aesthetics and Cultural Context* (New York: Columbia University Press, 2004), 193–194.

6. Bayton, "Women and the Electric Guitar," 48.

7. Steve Waksman, *Instruments of Desire: The Electric Guitar and the Shaping of Musical Experience* (Cambridge, Mass.: Harvard University Press, 1999), 6.

8. Robert Walser, *Running with the Devil: Power, Gender, and Madness in Heavy Metal Music* (Middletown, Conn.: Wesleyan University Press, 1993), 135.

9. Sherry Turkle, "Computational Reticence: Why Women Fear the Intimate Machine," in *Technology and Women's Voices: Keeping in Touch*, ed. Cheris Kramarae (New York: Routledge and Kegan Paul, 1988), 41.

10. Ibid., 44.

11. Ibid., 49.

12. Ibid., 50.

13. Ibid., 59.

14. B. B. King, album liner for *Lucille* (MCAD 10518), MCA Records Inc., Universal City, California, available online at http://www.worldblues.com/bbking/ prairie/lucille.html (accessed January 21, 2007).

15. Thanks to Annie Randall for her helpful insight on this issue.

16. To view the complete list, see *Rolling Stone*, "The Greatest Guitarists of all Time," http://www.rollingstone.com/news/story/5937559/the_100_greatest_guitarists_ of_all_time (accessed October 15, 2006).

17. David Segal, "No Girls Allowed? In the World of Guitar Boasts, Few Women Let Their Fingers Do the Walking," *Washington Post* (August 2004), http://www .washingtonpost.com/wp-dyn/articles/A19175-2004Aug20.html (accessed January 3, 2007).

18. Take, for instance, two overlooked female artists within the mainstream media, Sister Rosetta Tharpe and Carol Kaye. Tharpe was one of the first notable gospel recording artists in the 1930s and later was known for her innovative crossings of secular and sacred genres as she sang gospel music over her own electric guitar rock accompaniment. Tharpe influenced countless artists from Elvis Presley to Keith Richards to Johnny Cash. Electric bassist and guitarist Carol Kaye performed on countless hit songs, including The Beach Boys' "Good Vibrations," "Sloop John B" and "California Girls," Simon and Garfunkel's "Bridge Over Troubled Waters," The Carpenters' "(They Long to Be) Close to You," The Supremes' "Reflections," among many others. Despite their enormous talent and respect they earned from fellow musicians, Tharpe and Kaye are still marginalized by mainstream male authors within the popular music press. For more on these two noteworthy women, see Wikipedia, "Sister Rosetta Tharpe," http://en.wikipedia.org/wiki/Sister_Rosetta_ Tharpe and Wikipedia, "Carol Kaye," http://en.wikipedia.org/wiki/Carol_Kaye (both accessed January 20, 2007).

19. Mavis Bayton, "Women as Rock Musicians," in *On Record: Rock, Pop, and The Written Word*, ed. Simon Frith and Andrew Goodwin (New York: Pantheon Books, 1990), 238.

20. Fieldwork, of course, would be necessary to determine whether this theory is valid; I present it here as a possible topic for future research.

21. That Melissa Auf Der Maur, bassist for Hole in 1995 is Canadian was well documented in popular discourses; I was therefore compelled to identify this band as having "multiple" nationalities.

22. For tables 3.5 and 3.6 I am identifying band members' individual nationalities.

23. Although Morissette's harmonica was miked and amplified (like Nova's acoustic guitar) I consider both instruments to be acoustic here.

24. Paul Théberge, *Any Sound You Can Imagine: Making Music/Consuming Technology* (Middletown, Conn.: Wesleyan University Press, 1997), 4–5. I thank Jody Berland for bringing this to my attention.

25. Ibid., 120.

26. For a discussion of this pattern within the context of the Cuna, see Michael Taussig, *Mimesis and Alterity: A Particular History of the Senses* (New York: Routledge, 1993), 153–155. My thanks to Jody Berland for bringing this work to my attention.

27. See Beverley Diamond, "Gender, Music, Nation" (paper presented at the "Music and Nationalism" conference, at the Royal Irish Academy of Music, Dublin, September 1998).

28. Mackey, *The House of Difference*, 47.

29. Aaron Fox, "Alternative to What?: O Brother, September 11, and the Politics of 'Alternative' Country Music," in *There's a Star-Spangled Banner Waving Somewhere: Country Music Goes to War*, ed. Charles K. Wolfe and James E. Akenson (Lexington: University Press of Kentucky, 2004), 173.

30. For further analysis of this concert and the privileging of rock music discourses within Canada, see Susan Fast and Karen Pegley, "Music and Canadian Nationhood Post 9/11: An Analysis of *Music Without Borders: Live*," *Journal of Popular Music Studies* 18, no. 1 (2006): 18–39.

31. Goodwin, *Dancing in the Distraction Factory*, 136.

32. Marshall, *Celebrity and Power*, 193.

33. Of the 144 urban videos aired on MTV that week, 66 featured black female performers; 22, black male performers; and 56, mixed-gender groups.

34. To view this video go to http://www.youtube.com/watch?v=Yn6009 ZdIXY (accessed May 23, 2006).

35. One alternative video, "Tongue" by R.E.M., features the group performing on television. Because the audience is shown in small numbers, it is classified as a small-venue live performance context. To view this video go to http://www.you tube.com/watch?v=27m3caNwxCQ (accessed July 17, 2006).

36. "Buddy Holly" is an example of a small-venue format while simultaneously displaying Spike Jonze's virtuosity as a director. To view this video go to http://www .youtube.com/watch?v=sFaJpOgUPd8 (accessed August 13, 2005).

37. Marshall, *Celebrity and Power*, 195.

38. Ibid., 196.

39. Ibid.

40. Ibid.

41. Ibid., 195.

42. Gayle Wald, "Just a Girl? Rock Music, Feminism, and the Cultural Construction of Female Youth," *Signs* 23, no. 3 (1998): 608.

43. Catherine Driscoll, "Girl Culture, Revenge and Global Capitalism: Cybergirls, Riot Grrls, Spice Girls," *Australian Feminist Studies* 14, no. 29 (1999): 180.

44. According to Ray Cooper of Virgin Records, as cited in Richard C. Morais and Katherine Bruce, "What I wanna, wanna, really wannabe," *Forbes* (September 22, 1997): 186.

45. To view this video go to http://www.youtube.com/watch?v=VQbtm AaqvXs (accessed September 15, 2005).

46. Carter Harris, "Station Identification," *Vibe* 3/9 (November 1995): 76.

47. Harris, "Station Identification": 75.

48. The representation of the "absent" Canadian audience was also clear in Madonna's *Truth or Dare* documentary film of her "Blond Ambition" tour. The

scene shot within Toronto's Skydome featured Madonna onstage with two dancers performing provocatively, but the capacity audience is silhouetted with only a few individual arms seen waving against the stage backdrop.

49. Denise Donlon, interview by author, Toronto, Canada, October 29, 1998.

50. Greg Potter, *Hand Me Down World: The Canadian Pop-Rock Paradox* (Toronto: MacMillan, 1999), 3.

4. Multiculturalism, Diversity, and Containment (pp. 70–87)

1. Harris, "Station Identification," 75.

2. Richard Gold, "MTV Attitude Plays Big Role," *Variety* (December 15, 1982): 73.

3. Ibid., 75.

4. Cited in Serge Denisoff, *Inside MTV* (New Brunswick, N.J.: Tramsaction Publishers, 1989), 99.

5. Ibid., 102.

6. The interview is excerpted in ibid., 100–101.

7. Jane D. Brown, and Kenneth Campbell, "Race and Gender in Music Videos: The Same Beat but a Different Drummer," *Journal of Communication* 36, no. 1 (Winter 1986): 98.

8. Ibid., 104.

9. Cable began in the 1980s as a suburban luxury and it took time to connect urban centres, and inner-city neighborhoods. Once these links were established, *Yo! MTV Raps* began to achieve significantly higher ratings.

10. Goodwin, *Dancing in the Distraction Factory,* 137.

11. Homi Bhabha, "The Third Space. Interview with Homi Bhabha," in *Identity, Community, Culture, Difference,* ed. Jonathan Rutherford (London: Lawrence Wishart, 1990), 208.

12. Harris, "Station Identification," 76.

13. Ibid., 80.

14. CRTC Policy on Cultural Diversity, 1999–97, paragraph 115. Web site: www .crtc.gc.ca/archive/Notices/1999/PB99-97.htm (accessed June 6, 2005).

15. CRTC Decision 2000–138, paragraph 22. Web site: www.crtc.gc.ca/archive /Decisions/2000/DB2000-138.htm (accessed December 13, 2005).

16. Avi Lewis, interview by author, Toronto, Canada, November 6, 1998.

17. Rinaldo Walcott, *Black Like Who? Writing, Black, Canada* (Toronto: Insomniac Press, 1997), 83.

18. Ibid., 136.

19. To view this video go to http://www.youtube.com/watch?v=ZgiUqRpkSrE (accessed March 29, 2006).

20. This perception was both acknowledged and challenged by Maestro-Fresh Wes, who, after moving from Canada to the United States to further his career, released a record entitled *Naaah This Kid* Can't *Be From Canada* (1994). As Walcott points out, this title was intended to challenge the idea that the best rap songs were, and could only be, performed by African Americans (Walcott, *Black Like Who?* 91).

21. To view this video go to http://www.youtube.com/watch?v=Dlstɪn7z4Xk (February 14, 2006).

22. Rob Bowman, "Funk and James Brown: Re-Africanisation, the interlocked groove and the articulation of community" (paper presented at the Society for Ethnomusicology, Toronto, Ontario, October 1996), 3.

23. In his autobiography Brown states that he was not conscious of African music before he visited there: "I didn't even know it existed . . . [m]y roots may be imbedded in me and I don't know it, but when I went to Africa I didn't recognize

anything that I had gotten from there." In James Brown, Bruce Tucker, and Al Sharpton, *James Brown: The Godfather of Soul* (New York: Macmillan, 1986), 221.

24. Bowman, "Funk and James Brown," 2.

25. In fact, Brown was known for being an authoritarian figure with the band members; he was also arrested numerous times for personal assault against one of his wives. The real-life Brown was quite unlike the image he projected on stage and in videos.

26. To view this video go to http://www.youtube.com/watch?v=2bgwiQEdLAs (accessed October 11, 2006).

27. Robin Roberts, *Ladies First: Women in Music Videos* (Jackson: University Press of Mississippi, 1996), 166.

28. Chris Dafoe, "Rapping Latifah Rules New Tribes," *Toronto Star*, May 18, 1990, D8.

29. Roberts, *Ladies First*, 171.

30. Ibid., 166.

31. Ibid., 178.

32. George Lipsitz, *Dangerous Crossroads: Popular Music, Postmodernism and the Poetics of Place* (London: Verso, 1994), 25.

33. Timothy Brennan, *At Home in the World: Cosmopolitanism Now* (Cambridge, Mass.: Harvard University Press, 1997), 8. For more on this discussion, see 6–9.

34. Bhabha, "The Third Space," 221.

35. See Karen Pegley, "An Analysis of the Construction of National, Racial and Gendered Identities on MuchMusic (Canada) and MTV (US)" (Ph.D. diss., York University, 1999), 69–76.

36. D. Handelman, "Sold on Ice," *Rolling Stone* (January 10, 1991), cited by Goodwin, *Dancing in the Distraction Factory*, 106.

37. Patricia Hill Collins, *Black Sexual Politics: African Americans, Gender, and the New Racism* (New York: Routledge, 2004), 128.

38. Ibid., 29.

39. Lisa Lewis, *Gender Politics and MTV: Voicing the Difference* (Philadelphia: Temple University Press, 1990), 109.

40. To view this video go to http://www.youtube.com/watch?v=HuOhUa5GxAo (accessed August 4, 2006).

41. Lewis, *Gender Politics*, 121.

42. Ibid., 109.

43. To view this video go to http://www.youtube.com/watch?v=u_NCWrBoBNs (accessed February 25, 2006).

44. Lewis, *Gender Politics*, 119.

45. It is important to address briefly the problem of categorizing "Fantasy" as a video featuring a "white artist." Mariah Carey, in fact, is biracial: her father is a black Venezuelan and her mother is Irish Caucasian. Carey has made public references to her biracial background, sometimes counteracting music critics who have identified her as a white artist. For more on Carey's response, see Lynn Norent, "Mariah Carey: 'Not Just another White Girl Trying to Sing Black'" *Ebony* (March 1991), available online at: http://www.findarticles.com/p/articles/mi_m1077/is_n5_v46/ai_10405332 (accessed January 3, 2007). Despite Carey's efforts to identify as biracial, many in the popular music press identify her as white. She has been described, for instance, as Whitney Houston's (white) commercial rival in the female R&B market. As Amy Linden noted, "Mariah Carey . . . was presented to the record-buying public as a Long Island mall rat (you can read that as white);" Linden, "Smooth Operators: Contemporary R&B," in *Trouble Girls: The Rolling Stone Book of Women in Rock*, ed. Barbara O'Dair (New York: Random House, 1997), 389. It is therefore problematic to identify her as either white or black. To view this

video go to http://www.youtube.com/watch?v=ncRsj-G8oGE (accessed November 3, 2006).

46. To view this video go to http://www.youtube.com/watch?v=_NPvP 6oouao (accessed November 3, 2006).

47. To view this video go to http://www.youtube.com/watch?v=mQhm-meDit8 (accessed November 3, 2006).

48. To view this video go to http://www.youtube.com/watch?v=KWiOk-VkW2o (accessed November 3, 2006).

49. This video bears a striking resemblance to Michael Jackson's video "Black or White" wherein he evokes a series of cultural stereotypes. In particular, the Hollywood image of Native Americans is perpetuated by means of a "cowboys and Indians" fight.

50. Toni Morrison, *Playing in the Dark: Whiteness and the Literary Imagination* (Cambridge, Mass.: Harvard University Press, 1992), 67.

51. William Sonnega, "Morphing Borders," 49.

52. Ibid., 51.

53. Ibid.

54. Ibid.

55. Richard Dyer, *White* (New York: Routledge, 1997).

56. Ibid., 118–125.

57. To view this video go to http://www.youtube.com/watch?v=wU_tc8owVA8 (accessed November 5, 2006).

58. For more on these statistics, see http://www.everyhit.com/record5.html (accessed November 6, 2006).

59. To view this video go to http://www.youtube.com/watch?v=pGZCnGjKFS8 (accessed November 13, 2006).

60. That Adams is Canadian-born does not necessarily deem his music and videos "Canadian content." CRTC policy stipulates that a Canadian music video must include Canadian involvement in the audio component (the composition or performance of music and lyrics), and/or production (director, producer), and/or that production facilities be located within Canada. The detailed definition of a Canadian video clip is available online: http://www.crtc.gc.ca/archive/ENG/Notices/2000/PB2000–42.htm (accessed November 2, 2004). Adams's video did not meet the criteria.

61. Lucy Lippart, *Mixed Blessings: New Art in a Multicultural America* (New York: Pantheon Books, 1990), 26.

5. MuchMusic and MTV (pp. 88–103)

1. MuchUSA peaked with approximately 24 million viewers within the United States. It was sold to Rainbow Media in 2000 and is now called "Fuse."

2. "Seeing is Believing," http://www.seeingisbelieving.ca/cell/helsinki/ (accessed August 29, 2005).

3. Wikipedia, "Finland," http://en.wikipedia.org/wiki/Finland#_note-14 (accessed March 5, 2005).

4. Wikipedia, "Finland," http://en.wikipedia.org/wiki/Finland#Media_and_communications (accessed March 5, 2005).

5. Brett Dellinger, "Finnish Views of CNN Television News: A Critical Cross-Cultural Analysis of the American Commercial Discourse Style" (Ph.D. diss., ACTA Wasaensia No. 43, 1995), 25.

6. Ibid., 25–26.

7. Erja Ruohomaa, interview by author, Helsinki, Finland, August 1, 2000.

Ruohomaa was a researcher for the Finnish state-owned public radio and television company YLE.

8. "Scandinavia" is a highly ambiguous term. The Scandinavian countries officially are understood as Norway, Sweden, and Denmark, although Finland, the Faroe Islands, and Iceland are often unofficially counted as parts of Scandinavia. Because many of my informants understood Finland to be part of Scandinavia, it will be included under that label throughout my analysis.

9. For other models of cross-cultural media analyses, see Dellinger, "Finnish Views of CNN Television News"; and Daniel Hallin and Paolo Mancini, *Comparing Media Systems: Three Models of Media and Politics* (Cambridge: Cambridge University Press, 2004). These authors use television and news print as their primary texts, providing useful models for investigating cross-cultural media systems.

10. Taisto Hujanen, "Programming and Channel Competition in European Television," in *Television across Europe*, 65.

11. Richard J. Barnet and John Cavanagh, "Global Pop the sound of Money: Pop Imperialism Moves to a Global Beat," http://www.aislingmagazine.com/aisling magazine/articles/TAM25/GlobalPop.html (accessed April 5, 2005).

12. Jeremy Coopman and David Laing, "MTV Has Europe's Ear," *Variety* (August 26, 1991): 5, 103; and Steve Clarke, "Rock Conquers Continent," *Variety* (November 16, 1992): 35–36, as cited in Banks, *Monopoly Television*, 91.

13. Cited in "How MTV plays around the world," *New York Times*, July 7, 1991, sec. 2, p. 22.

14. Cited in Banks, *Monopoly Television*, 48.

15. Interview by author, Helsinki, Finland, July 20, 2000.

16. TVTV! was a cable station funded exclusively by advertising revenue, which meant that it was a free service for both the cable operators and viewers. It was sold and renamed "Subtv" in 2001 and is now an entertainment channel for teens and young adults.

17. Kristiina Werner, interview by author, Helsinki, Finland, July 20, 2000. Werner was *Jyrki*'s promotions director in 2000.

18. Harris M. Berger, "Introduction: The Politics and Aesthetics of Language Choice and Dialect in Popular Music," in *Global Pop, Local Language* (Jackson: University Press of Mississippi, 2003), x.

19. Finns, like Canadians, can apply to a fund for financial assistance when making a video. This source is ESEK, a granting agency that relies upon money earned from radio royalties. Artists reportedly receive a smaller grant if the video is sung in Finnish, but they don't need as much money as if it were in English.

20. Elli Suvaninen, interview by author, Helsinki, Finland, July 20, 2000.

21. Most of my informants were aware that feed comes from numerous sources. Several, however, felt that the information flow was unidirectional; as a result, Finns learned more about Canada but Canadians didn't learn about Finns. As one person observed: "I thought that Jyrki wasn't mentioned there [in Canada]." The observation that they were invisible to Canadian audiences was largely accurate.

22. Jordi Borja and Manuel Castells, *Local and Global: Management of Cities in the Information Age* (London: Earthscan, 1997), 203.

23. John Tomlinson, *Globalization and Culture* (Chicago: University of Chicago Press, 1999), 110.

24. Ibid., 109.

25. Ibid.

26. Néstor Garcia Canclini, *Hybrid Cultures: Strategies for Entering and Leaving Modernity*, trans. Renato Rosaldo (Minneapolis: University of Minnesota Press), 229.

27. Tomlinson, *Globalization and Culture*, 140.

28. Garcia Canclini, *Hybrid Cultures*, 234–235.

29. Marko Kulmala, e-mail message to author, April 30, 2007.

30. For the full entry see "MTV Finland," http://www.last.fm/user/meepu/journal/2005/09/18/15849/ (accessed November 25, 2006).

6. Conclusion (pp. 104–111)

1. Christopher John Farley. "Hip-Hop Nation," *Time* (February 8, 1999): 54–64.

2. Tom Henighan, *The Presumption of Culture: Structure, Strategy, and Survival in the Canadian Cultural Landscape* (Vancouver, B.C.: Raincoast Books, 1996), 52.

3. Henighan's insistence on hierarchical distinctions between "aesthetic" and "entertainment" forms is puzzling, particularly as on the following page he acknowledges, "the historical situation that has led us into a postmodern era in which many of the old boundaries between levels of culture are fast dissolving." See Henighan, *Presumption of Culture*, 53.

4. Walser, *Running with the Devil*, 111.

5. Interview with the author, Toronto, Canada, November 6, 1998.

6. Will Straw, "Much to Celebrate: A Decade of the Nation's Music Station," unpublished paper, 1994, p. 6.

Appendix A (pp. 115–123)

1. Goodwin, *Dancing in the Distraction Factory*, 140–141.

2. These nationality labels, of course, are highly problematic and should be regarded as such. For instance, Morissette, now living in the United States, arguably is regarded (by default) as American by many of her American fans, while more Canadians, because of media coverage, are aware of her country of origin. Canadian viewers of MuchMusic, then, are more likely to be privileged to this information than American MTV viewers (although access to information and knowledge about artists is not at all consistent). For this study, artists such as Morissette, Neil Young, Deborah Cox, and others were identified as Canadian, despite their current place of residence. Moreover, I chose to follow birthplace of the artist rather than Canadian content regulations to determine the degree of "Canadianness" of a video. Artists such as Bryan Adams or Alanis Morissette could be eliminated on such a basis and I do not believe these regulations reflect the perceptions of the Canadian viewing audience; that is, I believe that Colin James and Bryan Adams are perceived as Canadian by their fans, regardless of controversy surrounding their recording/production decisions.

3. I thank Annette Chrétien and Julie L'Heureux for their helpful translations of the more difficult Spanish and French videos.

4. Pegley, "'Much' Media," 38.

5. Shepherd, "Music and Male Hegemony," 154.

Bibliography

Adilman, Sid. "Yikes! They're tipping the cultural balance." *Toronto Star,* January 26, 1997, B1, B8.

Altman, Rick. "Television/Sound." In *Studies in Entertainment: Critical Approaches to Mass Culture,* edited by Tania Modleski, 39–54. Bloomington: Indiana University Press, 1986.

Anderson, Benedict. *Imagined Communities: Reflections on the Origin and Spread of Nationalism.* London: Verso, 1983.

Ang, Ien. "Culture and Communication: Towards an Ethnographic Critique of Media Consumption in the Transnational Media System." *European Journal of Communication* 5 (1990): 239–260.

——. *Living Room Wars: Rethinking Media Audiences for a Postmodern World.* London: Routledge, 1996.

Banks, Jack. "The Historical Development of the Video Music Industry: A Political Economic Analysis." Ph.D. diss., University of Oregon, 1991.

——. *Monopoly Television: MTV's Quest to Control the Music.* Boulder, Colo.: Westview, 1996.

Bayton, Mavis. "Women and the Electric Guitar." In *Sexing the Groove: Popular Music and Gender,* edited by Sheila Whiteley, 37–49. New York: Routledge, 1997.

——. "Women as Rock Musicians." In *On Record: Rock, Pop, and The Written Word,* edited by Simon Frith and Andrew Goodwin, 238–257. New York: Pantheon Books, 1990.

Berger, Harris M. "Introduction: The Politics and Aesthetics of Language Choice and Dialect in Popular Music." In *Global Pop, Local Language,* edited by Harris M. Berger and Michael Thomas Carroll, ix–xxvii. Jackson: University Press of Mississippi, 2003.

Berland, Jody. "Sound, Image and Social Space: Music Video and Media Reconstruction." In *Sound and Vision: The Music Video Reader,* edited by Simon Frith, Andrew Goodwin, and Lawrence Grossberg, 25–44. New York: Routledge, 1993.

——. "Space at the Margins: Colonial Spatiality and Critical Theory After Innis." *Topia* 1 (1997): 55–82.

Bessman, Jim. "MuchMusic is Much Different." *Billboard* 103 (1991): 63.

Bhabha, Homi. "The Third Space. Interview with Homi Bhabha." In *Identity, Community, Culture, Difference,* edited by Jonathan Rutherford, 207–221. London: Lawrence Wishart, 1990.

Boggs, Joseph. *The Art of Watching Films*. 3rd ed. Toronto: Addison-Wesley, 1991.

Borja, Jordi, and Manuel Castells. *Local and Global: Management of Cities in the Information Age*. London: Earthscan, 1997.

Bowman, Rob. "Funk and James Brown: Re-Africanisation, the interlocked groove and the articulation of community." Paper presented at the Society for Ethnomusicology, October, in Toronto, Ontario, 1996.

Brennan, Timothy. *At Home in the World: Cosmopolitan Now*. Cambridge, Mass.: Harvard University Press, 1997.

Bresba, Marco. Interview by author. Tape recording. Helsinki, Finland, July 20, 2000.

Brown, James, Bruce Tucker, and Al Sharpton. *James Brown: The Godfather of Soul*. New York: Macmillan, 1986.

Brown, Jane D., and Kenneth Campbell. "Race and Gender in Music Videos: The Same Beat but a Different Drummer." *Journal of Communication* 36, no. 1 (1986): 94–106.

Brown, Rich. "Tom Freston: The Pied Piper of Television." *Broadcasting and Cable* 124, no. 38 (1994): 36–40.

Butler, Judith. *Gender Trouble: Feminism and the Subversion of Identity*. New York: Routledge, 1990.

Callum, Fagan, Hickey, Kellog, Martinez, Schindler, and Schwartz. "TV Guide Presents 40 Years of the Best." *TV Guide* (April 1993): 92.

Canclini, Garcia, Néstor. *Hybrid Cultures: Strategies for Entering and Leaving Modernity*. Translated by Renato Rosaldo. Minneapolis: University of Minnesota Press, 1995.

Carnahan, Kerry. "Can Television Support an International Media Community? A Comparative Frame Analysis of MTV News in the United States and Europe." Master's thesis, University of Washington, 1994.

Carpenter, Carole. "The Ethnicity Factor in Anglo-Canadian Folklorists." In *Canadian Music: Issues of Hegemony and Identity*, edited by Beverley Diamond and Robert Witmer, 123–138. Toronto: Canadian Scholars' Press, 1994.

Cohen, Sara. "Men Making a Scene: Rock Music and the Production of Gender." In *Sexing the Groove: Popular Music and Gender*, edited by Sheila Whiteley, 17–33. New York: Routledge, 1997.

Collins, Richard. *Culture, Communication, and National Identity: The Case of Canadian Television*. Toronto: University of Toronto Press, 1990.

———. *Television: Policy and Culture*. London: Unwin Hyman, 1990.

Cubitt, Sean. *Timeshift: On Video Culture*. New York: Routledge, 1991.

Dafoe, Chris. "Rapping Latifah Rules New Tribes." *Toronto Star*, May 18, 1990, D8.

Danziger, Kurt. *Interpersonal Communication*. New York: Pergamon, 1976.

Day, Richard. "Constructing the Official Canadian: A Genealogy of the Mosaic Metaphor in State Policy Discourse." *Topia* 2 (1998): 42–66.

Dellinger, Brett. *Finnish Views of CNN Television News: A Critical Cross-Cultural Analysis of the American Commercial Discourse Style*. Vaasa, Finland: Universitas Wasaensis, 1995.

Denisoff, Serge. *Inside MTV*. New Brunswick, N.J.: Transaction Publishers, 1989.

Diamond, Beverley. "Gender, Music, Nation." Paper presented at the Music and National Conference, Royal Irish Academy of Music, Dublin, Ireland, September 1998.

Donlon, Denise. Interview by author. Tape recording. Toronto, Canada, October 29, 1998.

Driscoll, Catherine. "Girl Culture, Revenge and Global Capitalism: Cybergirls, Riot Grrls, Spice Girls." *Australian Feminist Studies* 12, no. 29 (1999): 173–195.

Dwyer, Leslie K. "Spectacular Society: Nationalism, Development and the Politics of Family Planning in Indonesia." In *Gender Ironies of Nationalism: Sexing the Nation,* edited by Tamar Mayer, 25–62. New York: Routledge, 2000.

Dyer, Richard. *White.* New York: Routledge, 1997.

Farley, Christopher John. "Hip-Hop Nation." *Time* (February 8, 1999): 54–64.

Fast, Susan, and Karen Pegley. "Music and Canadian Nationhood Post 9/11: An Analysis of *Music Without Borders: Live.*" *Journal of Popular Music Studies* 18, no. 1 (2006): 18–39.

Foucault, Michel. *The Archaeology of Knowledge.* Translated by A. M. Sheridan Smith. New York: Pantheon, 1972.

Fox, Aaron. "Alternative to What? O Brother, September 11, and the Politics of 'Alternative' Country Music." In *There's a Star-Spangled Banner Waving Somewhere: Country Music Goes to War,* edited by K. Wolfe and J. Akenson, 25–53. Lexington: University Press of Kentucky, 2004.

Frith, Simon. *Sound Effects: Youth, Leisure and the Politics of Rock 'n' Roll.* London: Constable, 1983.

———, Andrew Goodwin, and Lawrence Grossberg, eds. *Sound and Vision: The Music Video Reader.* New York: Routledge, 1993.

Goffman, Erving. *The Presentation of Self in Everyday Life.* Garden City, N.Y.: Doubleday, 1959.

Gold, Richard. "MTV Attitude Plays Big Role." *Variety* (December 15, 1995): 73.

Goodwin, Andrew. *Dancing in the Distraction Factory: Music Television and Popular Culture.* Minneapolis: University of Minnesota Press, 1992.

Hall, Stuart. "Cultural Identity and Diaspora." In *Identity, Community, Culture, Difference,* edited by Jonathan Rutherford, 232–237. London: Lawrence Wishart, 1990.

———. "The Question of Cultural Identity." In *Modernity: An Introduction to Modern Societies,* edited by Stuart Hall, David Held, Don Hubert, and Kenneth Thompson, 595–634. Cambridge: Open University Press, 1996.

Hallin, Daniel, and Paolo Mancini. *Comparing Media Systems: Three Models of Media and Politics.* Cambridge: Cambridge University Press, 2004.

Harris, Carter. "Station Identification." *Vibe* 3, no. 9 (1995): 75–76, 78, and 80.

Henighan, Tom. *The Presumption of Culture: Structure, Strategy, and Survival in the Canadian Cultural Landscape.* Vancouver: Raincoast Books, 1996.

Hill Collins, Patricia. *Black Sexual Politics: African Americans, Gender, and the New Racism.* New York: Routledge, 2004.

"How MTV plays around the world." *New York Times,* July 7, 1991, pp. 2 and 22.

Hujanen, Taisto. "Programming and Channel Competition in European Television." In *Television across Europe: A Comparative Introduction,* edited by Jan Wieten, Graham Murdock, and Peter Dahlgren, 65–83. London: Sage, 2000.

Innis, Harold. *The Bias of Communication.* Toronto: University of Toronto Press, 1951.

Kaplan, E. Ann. *Rocking Around the Clock: Music Television, Postmodernism, and Consumer Culture.* New York: Methuen, 1987.

Kinder, Marsha. "Music Video and the Spectator: Television, Ideology, and Dream." In *Television: The Critical View,* 4th ed., edited by Horace Newcomb, 229–254. London: Oxford University Press, 1987.

Kulmala, Marko. Interview by author. Tape recording. Helsinki, Finland, July 20, 2000.

Langer, John. "Television's Personality System." *Media, Culture and Society* 4 (1981): 351–365.

Lee, Jo-Anne, and John Lutz. "Introduction: Toward a Critical Literacy of Racisms, anti-Racisms, and Racialization. In *Situating "Race" and Racisms in Space, Time and Theory: Critical Essays for Activists and Scholars,* edited by Jo-Anne Lee and John Lutz, 3–29. Montreal and Kingston: McGill-Queen's University Press, 2005.

Lewis, Avi. Interview by the author. Tape recording. Toronto, Canada, November, 1998.

Lewis, Lisa. *Gender Politics and MTV: Voicing the Difference*. Philadelphia: Temple University Press, 1990.

Linden, Amy. "Smooth Operators: Contemporary R&B." In *Trouble Girls: The Rolling Stone Book of Women in Rock,* edited by Barbara O'Dair, 389–404. New York: Random House, 1997.

Lippart, Lucy. *Mixed Blessings: New Art in a Multicultural America*. New York: Pantheon, 1990.

Lipsitz, George. *Dangerous Crossroads: Popular Music, Postmodernism and the Poetics of Place*. London: Verso, 1994.

Mackey, Eva. *The House of Difference: Cultural Politics and National Identity in Canada*. Toronto: University of Toronto Press, 2002.

Marshall, David P. *Celebrity and Power: Fame in Contemporary Culture*. Minneapolis: University of Minnesota Press, 1997.

Mayer, Tamar. "Gender Ironies of Nationalism: Setting the Stage." In *Gender Ironies of Nationalism: Sexing the Nation*, edited by Tamar Mayer, 1–24. New York: Routledge, 2000.

McCarthy, Shawn. "Do we want cultural protection?" *Toronto Star,* February 1, 1997, F4.

McDonald, Marci. "A blow to magazines." *Macleans* (January 27, 1997): 58–59.

McRobbie, Angela, and Jenny Garber. "Girls and Subcultures." In *Feminism and Youth Culture: From "Jackie" to "Just Seventeen,"* 1–15. Boston: Unwin Hyman, 1991.

Meyerowitz, Joshua. *No Sense of Place: The Impact of Electronic Media on Social Behavior*. New York: Oxford University Press, 1985.

Morais, Richard C., and Katherine Bruce. "What I wanna, wanna, really wannabe." *Forbes* (September 22, 1997): 186.

Morley, David, and Kevin Robins. *Spaces of Identity: Global Media, Electronic Landscapes and Cultural Boundaries*. New York: Routledge, 1995.

Morrison, Toni. *Playing in the Dark Whiteness and the Literary Imagination*. Cambridge, Mass.: Harvard University Press, 1992.

Oikarinen, Olli. Interview by author. Tape recording. Helsinki, Finland, August 1, 2000.

Pegley, Karen. "An Analysis of the Construction of National, Racial and Gendered Identities on MuchMusic (Canada) and MTV (US)." Ph.D. diss., York University, 1999.

———. "'Much' Media: Towards an Understanding of the Impact of Music Videos on Canadian Pre-Adolescent Identities." *Canadian Folk Music Journal* 20 (1992): 33–39.

Potter, Greg. *Hand Me Down World: The Canadian Pop-Rock Paradox*. Toronto: Macmillan, 1999.

Potter, Russell A. *Spectacular Vernaculars: Hip-Hop and the Politics of Postmodernism*. Albany: State University of New York Press, 1995.

Probyn, Elspeth. *Outside Belongings*. New York: Routledge, 1996.

Renan, Ernest. "What is a Nation?" In *Nation and Narration,* edited by Homi Bhabha, 8–22. New York: Routledge, 1990.

Roberts, Robin. *Ladies First: Women in Music Videos*. Jackson: University Press of Mississippi, 1996.

Ruohomaa, Erja. Interview by author. Tape recording. Helsinki, Finland, August 1, 2000.

Sawchuck, Kim. "An Index of Power: Innis, Aesthetics, and Technology." In *Harold Innis in the New Century: Reflections and Refractions,* edited by C. Acland

and W. Buxton, 369–386. Montreal and Kingston: McGill-Queen's University Press, 1999.

Schlesinger, Philip. "On National Identity: Some Conceptions and Misconceptions Criticized." *Social Science Information* 26, no. 2 (1987): 219–264.

Shales, Tom. "The Pop Network That's Dim and Ditzy to Decor." *Washington Post*, August 1, 1985, B9.

Shepherd, John. "Music and Male Hegemony." In *Music and Society: The Politics of Composition, Performance and Reception,* edited by Richard Leppert and Susan McClary, 151–172. Cambridge: Cambridge University Press, 1992.

Shuker, Roy. *Understanding Popular Music,* 2nd ed. New York: Routledge, 2001.

Sonnega, William. "Morphing Borders: The Remanence of MTV." *Drama Review* 39, no. 1 (1995): 45–61.

Straw, Will. "Much to Celebrate: A Decade of the Nation's Music Station." 1994.

Strinati, Dominic. *An Introduction to Theories of Popular Culture.* New York: Routledge, 1995.

Suvaninen, Elli. Interview by author. Tape recording. Helsinki, Finland, July 20, 2000.

Taussig, Michael. *Mimesis and Alterity: A Particular History of the Senses.* New York: Routledge, 1993.

Théberge, Paul. *Any Sound You Can Imagine: Making Music/Consuming Technology.* Middletown, Conn.: Wesleyan University Press, 1997.

Tobenkin, David. "The all-music channels." *Broadcasting and Cable* 2 (September 1996): 38–44.

Tomlinson, John. *Globalization and Culture.* Chicago: University of Chicago Press, 1999.

Turkle, Sherry. "Computational Reticence: Why Women Fear the Intimate Machine." In *Technology and Women's Voices: Keeping in Touch,* edited by Cheris Kramarae, 41–61. New York: Routledge and Kegan Paul, 1988.

Vernallis, Carol. *Experiencing Music Video: Aesthetics and Cultural Context.* New York: Columbia University Press, 2004.

Wagman, Ira. "Rock the Nation: MuchMusic, Cultural Policy and the Development of English-Canadian Music-Video Programming, 1979–1984." *Canadian Journal of Communication* 26, no. 4 (2001): 503–518.

Walcott, Rinaldo. *Black Like Who? Writing, Black, Canada.* Toronto: Insomniac Press, 1997.

Wald, Gayle. "Just a Girl? Rock Music, Feminism, and the Cultural Construction of Female Youth." *Signs* 23, no. 3 (1998): 585–610.

Weber, Robert. *Basic Content Analysis.* Beverly Hills, Calif.: Sage Publications, 1985.

Walser, Robert. *Running with the Devil: Power, Gender, and Madness in Heavy Metal Music.* Middletown, Conn.: Wesleyan University Press, 1993.

Werner, Kristiina. Interview by author. Tape recording. Helsinki, Finland, July 20, 2000.

Winston, Brian. "On Counting the Wrong Things." In *The Media Reader,* edited by Manuel Alvarado and John O. Thompson, 50–64. London: British Film Institute, 1990.

Williams, Kevin. "Musical Visuality: A Phenomenological Essay on Music Television." Ph.D. diss., Ohio University, 1995.

Williams, Raymond. *Television: Technology and Cultural Form.* New York: Schocken Books, 1975.

Williams, Steven. "An Analysis of Social Critique in Music Videos Broadcast on MuchMusic." Master's thesis, University of Alberta, 1993.

Index

❧

Page numbers in italics refer to tables or photographs

Hall, Stuart, 7–8, 104
Halliwell, Geri, 64
"Hand In My Pocket" (Alanis Morissette), 48, 49, 50, 57
Hanna, Kathleen, 54
"Hard as a Rock" (AC/DC), 67
"Hard Times" (Queen Latifah), 49
harmonicas, 51
Harris, Carter, 67, 70, 72
Harrison, George, 77
Hatfield, Juliana, 50
"Have You Ever Really Loved A Woman?" (Bryan Adams), 84–86, 109, 142n60
Helsinki, Finland, 101
Hendrix, Jimi, 53–54
Henighan, Tom, 108–9, 144n3 (Chap. 6)
hierarchical structures. See class
high culture, 13, 109
hip hop, 4, 74, 82
Hole, 49, 49, 50, 51, 56–57, 65
"Hook" (Blues Travelers), 120
"Hooked on You" (Silk), 80–82, 81
Hootie and the Blowfish, 67
household flow: overview, 23, 27–31; MTV manipulation of, 105; sound as component of, 27–28; time-space media bias and, 43; verbal text and, 136–37n7
Houston, Whitney, 141n45
"Hurt" (Nine Inch Nails), 63
hybridity, 8

"Ice Ice Baby" (Vanilla Ice), 77
Idalis, 33
"I'll Stick Around" (Foo Fighters), 122
imagined community: defined, 4; commercials and, 42; individual vs. collective audience and, 4, 42–43, 105, 133n6; station audiences and, 5
indie music, 54
individualism, 4, 42–43, 105, 133n6
Innis, Harold, 20, 42–44
Internet, 15, 18
Intimate and Interactive, 34, 36–37, 43
invisible audiences, 68, 139–40n48
Isaak, Chris, 33, 81, 81
"I've Got My Mind Set On You" (George Harrison), 77
"I Wanna Touch You" (Def Leppard), 67
"I Will Make Love to You" (Boyz II Men), 11
"I Will Remember You" (Sarah McLaughlin), 50
"I Wish" (The Misunderstood), 50

Jackass, 17
Jackson, Janet, 10, 81, 82–83, 86, 107, 109
Jackson, Luscious, 39
Jackson, Michael, 40, 71, 83–84
James, Colin, 144n2 (Appendix A)
James, Rick, 70
"Janie's Got a Gun" (Aerosmith), 11
jazz music, 59, 70
Jazzy Jeff, 67
Jett, Joan, 54
Jones, Quincy, 74
Jonze, Spike, 139n36
Juke Box, 30
Jyrki (Finland): overview, 21, 88–89; deterritorialization and, 101–3; failure of, 102–3; MuchMusic influence on, 3, 96–97, 98–99; regionalizing influence of, 95–97, 107–8

"Kashmir" (The Ordinaires), 50
Kaye, Carol, 138n18
Kelly, R., 81, 81
Kennedy, 32–33, 33
keyboard instruments, 51
Killah Priest, 33, 37
King, B. B., 53
"Kool Thing" (Sonic Youth), 50
Kulmala, Marko, 94

L7, 50
"Ladies First" (Queen Latifah), 10, 75–76
lang, k. d., 59, 68, 108
Langer, John, 31–33
language: coding of, 119; English vs. Finnish programming in Finland, 91–92, 96–99; French-language pop rock, 25–26; in station repertoires, 39
Lauper, Cyndi, 80
Lavigne, Avril, 59
Lee, Jo-Ann, 8
Lee, Sook-Yin, 34, 34, 35
Left Eye (Lisa Lopes), 65–66
Lewis, Avi, 73, 110
Lewis, Lisa, 79–80, 83
Lightfoot, Gordon, 59, 108–9
Linden, Amy, 141n45
Lippard, Lucy, 86
Lipsitz, George, 76
Little, Suzanne, 50
live performance videos: articulation of community in, 75; coding of, 121–22; importance in metal music, 60–61; "live" definition, 137n2; men as subjects

136–37n7; ideological motives in, 2; lifestyle programming, 17; live performances, 36–38, *37*; programming flow, 25–26; ratings and, 17; "softening" of music by black artists, 67, 71–73, 106–7; time zones and, 32, 34–35; women instrumentalists and, 48–55, *49–50*, *52*

protectionism: "Canadian content" requirement, 12, 16, 46, 49, 86, 134n11; Canadian regulatory environment and, 3, 5; split-run magazines, 12–13

public broadcasting, 24, 26, 31

Public Enemy, 74

punk rock music, 54, 71

"Push It" (Salt-N-Pepa), 10, *49*, 63

Queen Latifah, 10, *49*, 75–77

race: defined, 8–9; Afrocentricity, 74–76; bias in video programming, 2, 5, 21, 70–77, 106–7; coding of, 118; in dance videos, 77–84, *78*, *81*, *87*; in "Fantasy," 141n45; multiculturalist paradigm and, 6–7, 72; "softening" of music by black artists, 67, 71–73, 106–7; stereotypes and, 83; urban music live performance and, 63–64, 66; whiteness as normative, 84–86

Rainbow Media, 4

Raitt, Bonnie, *50*, 51, 56, 67

Rap City, 25, 30, 76

rap music: defined, 9; as American genre, 74, 82, 140n20; gangsta rap music, 67; marketing techniques of black artists, 65; in MTV repertoire, 2, 71–73, 106–7; in MuchMusic repertoire, 74; political critique in, 74–77; "softening" of imagery of, 66–67, 71–73, 106–7. See also *Rap City*

ratings, 17, 27, 30–31

Raymond, Francine, *50*, 51

Real World, The, 17

"Red Light Special" (TLC), 65–66

"Red Red Wine" (UB40), 40

"Reflections" (Supremes), 138n18

reggae music, 72–73, 76–77, 107

Reggae Sound System, 72–73, 76–77

regionalization. *See* localization

R.E.M., 77, 139n35

Renan, Ernest, 6

Rentals, the, *49*

repertoire. *See* programming

Rex, Simon, 32, *33*

Richard, Natalie, *34*, 35

Richards, Keith, 138n18

riot grrl movement, 65

Road Rules, 25

Robert Burton and the Strange, *50*

Roberts, Robin, 75

Robin Hood, Prince of Thieves, 85

Robins, Kevin, 19

Rock, Chris, 66

"Rocket" (Smashing Pumpkins), *49*

rock music: defined, 9–10; female vocalists vs. instrumentalists in, 46–48; male dominance in, 45, 52, 54–55, 138n18; in MTV repertoire, 106; as symbol of Canadian identity, 59–60

"Rock Steady" (Bonnie Raitt and Bryan Adams), *50*, 56, 67

Rolling Stone magazine, 54, 70

Rolling Stones, 64

Roncon, Teresa, *34*

Ross, Bob, 41

R.S.V.P., *34*

Rude Awakening, 32, *33*

"Runaway" (Bon Jovi), 40

"Runaway" (Janet Jackson), 10, *81*, 82–83, 86, 109

Run-D.M.C., 71

Rusted Root, *50*

Salt-N-Pepa, 10, *33*, *49*, 63, *81*, 81–83

Sawchuck, Kim, 43

Schlesinger, Philip, 19–20

Segal, David, 54

Sencio, John, 32, *33*, 34

"Sentimental" (Deborah Cox), 63

Sex Pistols, 64

sexuality: commoditized sexuality in dance, 79, 87, 106; in rock guitar videography, 47; sexual simulation in rock guitar performance, 53–54; TLC sexual imagery, 65–66

Shepherd, John, 36, 122

"She's Strange" (Cameo), 40

"Shocker in the Gloomroom" (The Breeders), *50*

"Sho Nuff Funky" (Afrika Bambaataa), 75–76

Shuker, Roy, 9

silence, 28–29, 120, 136–37n7

Silk, 80–82, *81*

Silverchair, 122

Simon and Garfunkle, 138n18

Singled Out, 25

Weeping Tile, 48, *50*, *55*
Weezer, 63, 139n36
Welychka, Bill, 30, *34*
Werner, Kristiina, 96
"What a Life" (Juliana Hatfield), *50*
"When Love and Hate Collide" (Def Leppard), 121
whiteness, 84–86
White Zombies, *49*
"Who Can I Run To" (Xscape), 63
"Wild Country" (Robert Burton and the Strange), *50*
Williams, Kevin, 135n48
Williams, Raymond, 24, 26, 27, 116–17
Williams, Steven, 14, 118–23, 135n48
Winston, Brian, 14
women: on acoustic vs. electric instruments, 48, 51, 55, 57, 60, 69, 138n18; in dance videos, 77–84, *78, 81*, 87; "girl power" phenomenon, 65–66; as instrumentalists vs. vocalists, 21, 46–48; as music video instrumentalists, 48–55, *49–50, 52*; nationality of female video instrumentalists, 55–58, *56–58*; "softening" of rap music and, 67, 106–7; technology and, 52–53; "third-wave feminism," 66; videographic composition of, 47–48. *See also* gender
Wretzky, D'arcy, 48

Xscape, *33*, 63

Yack Live, 30
Yo! MTV Raps, 66–67, 71–73, 107, 140n9
Young, Neil, 67–68, 109
"You Remind Me of Something" (R. Kelly), *81*, 81
"Your Little Secret" (Melissa Etheridge), 11, 48, *49*
YouTube, 18

Z Music Television, 40
Znaimer, Moses, 5, 108

MUSIC/CULTURE

A series from Wesleyan University Press

Edited by Harris M. Berger and Annie J. Randall

Originating editors: George Lipsitz, Susan McClary, and Robert Walser.

Listening to Salsa:
Gender, Latin Popular Music, and
Puerto Rican Cultures
by Frances Aparicio

Jazz Consciousness: Music, Race, and
Humanity
by Paul Austerlitz

Metal, Rock, and Jazz:
Perception and the Phenomenology Mu-
sical Experience
by Harris M. Berger

Identity and Everyday Life:
Essays in the Study of Folklore, Music
and Popular Culture
by Harris M. Berger and Giovanna P.
Del Negro

Bright Balkan Morning:
Romani Lives and the Power of Music
in Greek Macedonia
by Dick Blau and Charles and
Angeliki Keil

Different Childhoods:
Music and the Cultures of Youth
edited by Susan Boynton and
Roe-Min Kok

Music and Cinema
edited by James Buhler, Caryl Flinn,
and David Neumeyer

My Music
by Susan D. Crafts, Daniel Cavicchi,
Charles Keil, and the Music in Daily
Life Project

Born in the USA:
Bruce Springsteen and the American
Tradition
by Jim Cullen

Presence and Pleasure:
The Funk Grooves of James Brown and
Parliament
by Anne Danielsen

Echo and Reverb:
Fabricating Space in Popular Music
1900–1960
by Peter Doyle

Recollecting from the Past:
Musical Practice and Spirit Possession on
the East Coast of Madagascar
by Ron Emoff

Locating East Asia in Western Art
Music
edited by Yayoi Uno Everett and
Frederick Lau

Black Rhythms of Peru:
Reviving African Musical Heritage in
the Black Pacific
by Heidi Feldman

"You Better Work!":
Underground Dance Music in New
York City
by Kai Fikentscher

The Hidden Musicians:
Music-Making in an English Town
by Ruth Finnegan

Musicking:
The Meanings of Performing and
Listening
by Christopher Small

Music of the Common Tongue:
Survival and Celebration in African
American Music
by Christopher Small

Singing Our Way to Victory:
French Cultural Politics and Music
During the Great War
by Regina M. Sweeney

Setting the Record Straight: A Material
History of Classical Recording
by Colin Symes

False Prophet:
Fieldnotes from the Punk Underground
by Steven Taylor

Any Sound You Can Imagine:
Making Music/Consuming Technology
by Paul Théberge

Club Cultures:
Music, Media and Sub-cultural Capital
by Sarah Thornton

Dub:
Songscape and Shattered Songs in
Jamaican Reggae
by Michael E. Veal

Running with the Devil:
Power, Gender, and Madness in Heavy
Metal Music
by Robert Walser

Manufacturing the Muse:
Estey Organs and Consumer Culture in
Victorian America
by Dennis Waring

The City of Musical Memory:
Salsa, Record Grooves, and Popular
Culture in Cali, Colombia
by Lise A. Waxer

ABOUT THE AUTHOR

Kip Pegley is Associate Professor
Music at Queen's University in C